Wonderful ways to prepare

CHEESECAKES

by JO ANN SHIRLEY

Wonderful ways to prepare
CHEESECAKES

PLAYMORE INC. NEW YORK USA
UNDER ARRANGEMENT WITH
WALDMAN PUBLISHING CORP.

AYERS & JAMES
SYDNEY AUSTRALIA

STAFFORD PEMBERTON PUBLISHING
KNUTSFORD UNITED KINGDOM

FIRST PUBLISHED 1979

PUBLISHED IN THE USA
BY PLAYMORE INC.
UNDER ARRANGEMENT WITH
WALDMAN PUBLISHING CORP.

PUBLISHED IN AUSTRALIA
BY AYERS & JAMES
CROWS NEST. AUSTRALIA

PUBLISHED IN THE UNITED KINGDOM
BY STAFFORD PEMBERTON PUBLISHING
KNUTSFORD CHESHIRE

ISBN 0 86908 160 8

OVEN TEMPERATURE GUIDE

Description	Gas		Electric		Mark
	C	F	C	F	
Cool	100	200	110	225	¼
Very Slow	120	250	120	250	½
Slow	150	300	150	300	1-2
Moderately slow	160	325	170	340	3
Moderate	180	350	200	400	4
Moderately hot	190	375	220	425	5-6
Hot	200	400	230	450	6-7
Very hot	230	450	250	475	8-9

LIQUID MEASURES

IMPERIAL	METRIC
1 teaspoon	5 ml
1 tablespoon	20 ml
2 fluid ounces (½ cup)	62.5 ml
4 fluid ounces (½ cup)	125 ml
8 fluid ounces (1 cup)	250 ml
1 pint (16 ounces — 2 cups)*	500 ml

* (The imperial pint is equal to 20 fluid ounces.)

SOLID MEASURES

AVOIRDUPOIS	METRIC
1 ounce	30 g
4 ounces (¼ lb)	125 g
8 ounces (½ lb)	250 g
12 ounces (¾ lb)	375 g
16 ounces (1 lb)	500 g
24 ounces (1½ lb)	750 g
32 ounces (2 lb)	1000 g (1 kg)

CUP AND SPOON REPLACEMENTS FOR OUNCES

INGREDIENT	½ oz	1 oz	2 oz	3 oz	4 oz	5 oz	6 oz	7 oz	8 oz
Almonds, ground	2 T	¼ C	½ C	¾ C	1¼ C	1⅓ C	1⅔ C	2 C	2¼ C
slivered	6 t	¼ C	½ C	¾ C	1 C	1⅓ C	1⅔ C	2 C	2¼ C
whole	2 T	¼ C	⅓ C	½ C	¾ C	1 C	1¼ C	1⅓ C	1½ C
Apples, dried whole	3 T	½ C	1 C	1⅓ C	2 C	2⅓ C	2¾ C	3⅓ C	3¾ C
Apricots, chopped	2 T	¼ C	½ C	¾ C	1 C	1¼ C	1½ C	1¾ C	2 C
whole	2 T	3 T	½ C	⅔ C	1 C	1¼ C	1⅓ C	1½ C	1¾ C
Arrowroot	1 T	2 T	⅓ C	½ C	⅔ C	¾ C	1 C	1¼ C	1⅓ C
Baking Powder	1 T	2 T	⅓ C	½ C	⅔ C	¾ C	1 C	1 C	1¼ C
Baking Soda	1 T	2 T	⅓ C	½ C	⅔ C	¾ C	1 C	1 C	1¼ C
Barley	1 T	2 T	¼ C	½ C	⅔ C	¾ C	1 C	1 C	1¼ C
Breadcrumbs, dry	2 T	¼ C	½ C	¾ C	1 C	1¼ C	1½ C	1¾ C	2 C
soft	¼ C	½ C	1 C	1½ C	2 C	2½ C	3 C	3⅔ C	4¼ C
Biscuit Crumbs	2 T	¼ C	½ C	¾ C	1¼ C	1⅓ C	1⅔ C	2 C	2¼ C
Butter	3 t	6 t	¼ C	⅓ C	½ C	⅔ C	¾ C	1 C	1 C
Cheese, grated, lightly packed,									
natural cheddar	6 t	¼ C	½ C	¾ C	1 C	1¼ C	1½ C	1¾ C	2 C
Processed cheddar	5 t	2 T	⅓ C	⅔ C	¾ C	1 C	1¼ C	1½ C	1⅔ C
Parmesan, Romano	6 t	¼ C	½ C	¾ C	1 C	1⅓ C	1⅔ C	2 C	2¼ C
Cherries, candied, chopped	1 T	2 T	⅓ C	½ C	¾ C	1 C	1 C	1⅓ C	1½ C
whole	1 T	2 T	⅓ C	½ C	⅔ C	¾ C	1 C	1¼ C	1⅓ C
Cocoa	2 T	¼ C	½ C	¾ C	1¼ C	1⅓ C	1⅔ C	2 C	2¼ C
Coconut, desiccated	2 T	⅓ C	⅔ C	1 C	1⅓ C	1⅔ C	2 C	2⅓ C	2⅔ C
shredded	⅓ C	⅔ C	1¼ C	1¾ C	2½ C	3 C	3⅔ C	4⅓ C	5 C
Cornstarch	6 t	3 T	½ C	⅔ C	1 C	1¼ C	1½ C	1⅔ C	2 C
Corn Syrup	2 t	1 T	2 T	¼ C	⅓ C	½ C	½ C	⅔ C	⅔ C
Coffee, ground	2 T	⅓ C	⅔ C	1 C	1⅓ C	1⅔ C	2 C	2⅓ C	2⅔ C
instant	3 T	½ C	1 C	1⅓ C	1¾ C	2¼ C	2⅔ C	3 C	3½ C
Cornflakes	½ C	1 C	2 C	3 C	4¼ C	5¼ C	6¼ C	7⅓ C	8⅓ C
Cream of Tartar	1 T	2 T	⅓ C	½ C	⅔ C	¾ C	1 C	1 C	1¼ C
Currants	1 T	2 T	⅓ C	⅔ C	¾ C	1 C	1¼ C	1½ C	1⅔ C
Custard Powder	6 t	3 T	½ C	⅔ C	1 C	1¼ C	1½ C	1⅔ C	2 C
Dates, chopped	1 T	2 T	⅓ C	⅔ C	¾ C	1 C	1¼ C	1½ C	1⅔ C
whole, pitted	1 T	2 T	⅓ C	½ C	¾ C	1 C	1¼ C	1⅓ C	1½ C
Figs, chopped	1 T	2 T	⅓ C	½ C	¾ C	1 C	1 C	1⅓ C	1½ C
Flour, all-purpose or cake	6 t	¼ C	½ C	¾ C	1 C	1¼ C	1½ C	1¾ C	2 C
wholemeal	6 t	3 T	½ C	⅔ C	1 C	1¼ C	1⅓ C	1⅔ C	1¾ C
Fruit, mixed	1 T	2 T	⅓ C	½ C	¾ C	1 C	1¼ C	1⅓ C	1½ C
Gelatin	5 t	2 T	⅓ C	½ C	¾ C	1 C	1 C	1¼ C	1½ C
Ginger, crystallised pieces	1 T	2 T	⅓ C	½ C	¾ C	1 C	1¼ C	1⅓ C	1½ C
ground	6 t	⅓ C	½ C	¾ C	1¼ C	1½ C	1¾ C	2 C	2¼ C
preserved, heavy syrup	1 T	2 T	⅓ C	½ C	⅔ C	¾ C	1 C	1 C	1¼ C
Glucose, liquid	2 t	1 T	2 T	¼ C	⅓ C	½ C	½ C	⅔ C	⅔ C
Haricot Beans	1 T	2 T	⅓ C	½ C	⅔ C	¾ C	1 C	1 C	1¼ C

In this table, t represents teaspoonful, T represents tablespoonful and C represents cupful.

CUP AND SPOON REPLACEMENTS FOR OUNCES (Cont.)

INGREDIENT	½ oz	1 oz	2 oz	3 oz	4 oz	5 oz	6 oz	7 oz	8 oz
Honey	2 t	1 T	2 T	¼ C	⅓ C	½ C	½ C	⅔ C	⅔ C
Jam	2 t	1 T	2 T	¼ C	⅓ C	½ C	½ C	⅔ C	¾ C
Lentils	1 T	2 T	⅓ C	½ C	⅔ C	¾ C	1 C	1 C	1¼ C
Macaroni (see pasta)									
Milk Powder, full cream	2 T	¼ C	½ C	¾ C	1¼ C	1⅓ C	1⅔ C	2 C	2¼ C
non fat	2 T	⅓ C	¾ C	1¼ C	1½ C	2 C	2⅓ C	2¾ C	3¼ C
Nutmeg	6 t	3 T	½ C	⅔ C	¾ C	1 C	1¼ C	1½ C	1⅔ C
Nuts, chopped	6 t	¼ C	½ C	¾ C	1 C	1¼ C	1½ C	1¾ C	2 C
Oatmeal	1 T	2 T	½ C	⅔ C	¾ C	1 C	1¼ C	1½ C	1⅔ C
Olives, whole	1 T	2 T	⅓ C	⅔ C	¾ C	1 C	1¼ C	1½ C	1⅔ C
sliced	1 T	2 T	⅓ C	⅔ C	¾ C	1 C	1¼ C	1½ C	1⅔ C
Pasta, short (e.g. macaroni)	1 T	2 T	⅓ C	⅔ C	¾ C	1 C	1¼ C	1½ C	1⅔ C
Peaches, dried & whole	1 T	2 T	⅓ C	⅔ C	¾ C	1 C	1¼ C	1½ C	1⅔ C
chopped	6 t	¼ C	½ C	¾ C	1 C	1¼ C	1½ C	1¾ C	2 C
Peanuts, shelled, raw, whole	1 T	2 T	⅓ C	½ C	¾ C	1 C	1¼ C	1⅓ C	1½ C
roasted	1 T	2 T	⅓ C	⅔ C	¾ C	1 C	1¼ C	1½ C	1⅔ C
Peanut Butter	3 t	6 t	3 T	⅓ C	½ C	½ C	⅔ C	¾ C	1 C
Peas, split	1 T	2 T	⅓ C	½ C	⅔ C	¾ C	1 C	1 C	1¼ C
Peel, mixed	1 T	2 T	⅓ C	½ C	¾ C	1 C	1 C	1¼ C	1½ C
Potato, powder	1 T	2 T	¼ C	⅓ C	½ C	⅔ C	¾ C	1 C	1¼ C
flakes	¼ C	½ C	1 C	1⅓ C	2 C	2⅓ C	2¾ C	3⅓ C	3¾ C
Prunes, chopped	1 T	2 T	⅓ C	½ C	⅔ C	¾ C	1 C	1¼ C	1⅓ C
whole pitted	1 T	2 T	⅓ C	½ C	⅔ C	¾ C	1 C	1 C	1¼ C
Raisins	2 T	¼ C	⅓ C	½ C	¾ C	1 C	1 C	1⅓ C	1½ C
Rice, short grain, raw	1 T	2 T	¼ C	½ C	⅔ C	¾ C	1 C	1 C	1¼ C
long grain, raw	1 T	2 T	⅓ C	½ C	¾ C	1 C	1¼ C	1⅓ C	1½ C
Rice Bubbles	⅔ C	1¼ C	2½ C	3⅔ C	5 C	6¼ C	7½ C	8¾ C	10 C
Rolled Oats	2 T	⅓ C	⅔ C	1 C	1⅓ C	1¾ C	2 C	2½ C	2¾ C
Sago	2 T	¼ C	⅓ C	½ C	¾ C	1 C	1 C	1¼ C	1½ C
Salt, common	3 t	6 t	¼ C	⅓ C	½ C	⅔ C	¾ C	1 C	1 C
Semolina	1 T	2 T	⅓ C	½ C	¾ C	1 C	1 C	1⅓ C	1½ C
Spices	6 t	3 T	¼ C	⅓ C	½ C	½ C	⅔ C	¾ C	1 C
Sugar, plain	3 t	6 t	¼ C	⅓ C	½ C	⅔ C	¾ C	1 C	1 C
confectioners'	1 T	2 T	⅓ C	½ C	¾ C	1 C	1 C	1¼ C	1½ C
moist brown	1 T	2 T	⅓ C	½ C	¾ C	1 C	1 C	1⅓ C	1½ C
Tapioca	1 T	2 T	⅓ C	½ C	⅔ C	¾ C	1 C	1¼ C	1⅓ C
Treacle	2 t	1 T	2 T	¼ C	⅓ C	½ C	½ C	⅔ C	⅔ C
Walnuts, chopped	2 T	¼ C	½ C	¾ C	1 C	1¼ C	1½ C	1¾ C	2 C
halved	2 T	⅓ C	⅔ C	1 C	1¼ C	1½ C	1¾ C	2¼ C	2½ C
Yeast, dried	6 t	3 T	½ C	⅔ C	1 C	1¼ C	1⅓ C	1⅔ C	1¾ C
compressed	3 t	6 t	3 T	⅓ C	½ C	½ C	⅔ C	¾ C	1 C

In this table, t represents teaspoonful, T represents tablespoonful and C represents cupful.

Contents

Cheesecakes

Neopolitan Cake

Cake:
4 eggs
1 cup sugar
2 cups cake flour
⅛ teaspoon salt
3 tablespoons (45 g) butter
1 cup (250 ml) warm milk
1½ teaspoons vanilla essence
3 drops red food coloring
2½ tablespoons cocoa
2½ tablespoons warm milk

Filling:
2 egg whites
1 cup confectioner's sugar
⅔ cup (165 g) butter

Frosting:
¼ lb (125 g) cream cheese
2 tablespoons milk
½ teaspoon vanilla essence
4 cups confectioner's sugar
2 drops red food coloring

1. Beat the eggs well. Add the sugar and continue beating until light and fluffy.
2. Sift the flour with the salt and add to the egg mixture.
3. Mix the butter with the warm milk until melted and add to the flour-egg mixture with the vanilla essence. Mix gently but thoroughly.
4. Divide the cake mixture into three equal portions. Mix the red food coloring into one. Mix the cocoa with the warm milk and add to the second portion. Leave the third portion plain.
5. Butter and flour three 8-inch (20-cm) cake tins and pour in the three portions. Bake in a 350°F (180°C) oven for about 25 minutes. Cool slightly, then turn out.
6. Mix the egg whites and the confectioner's sugar in the top of a double boiler. Put over hot water and beat until firm. Remove from heat and continue to beat until stiff.
7. Cream the butter until very soft. Fold into the egg white mixture.
8. Spread between cake layers.
9. Mix together the cream cheese, milk and vanilla until soft and smooth.
10. Slowly add the sifted confectioner's sugar and mix until thoroughly blended. Add the coloring and spread on the top and sides of the cake.

Serves 8-10.

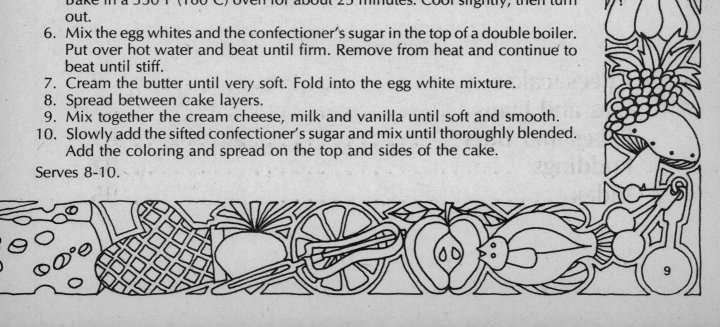

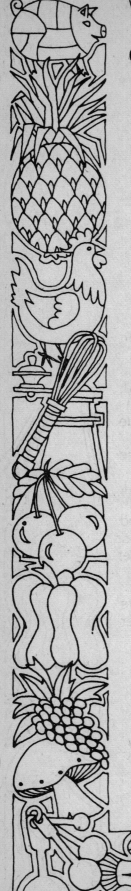

German Cheesecake

Pastry:
1 cup plain flour
½ teaspoon salt
⅓ cup (85 g) butter
3 tablespoons cold water

Filling:
375 g (¾ lb) cream cheese
½ cup sugar
3 eggs
1 teaspoon vanilla essence

Sultana Raisin Topping:
1½ cups (265 g) sultana raisins
½ cup sugar
½ cup (125 ml) milk
2 teaspoons grated lemon rind
1 teaspoon vanilla essence

Crumble Topping:
½ cup plain flour
5 tablespoons (85 g) butter
½ cup brown sugar

1. Sift the flour with the salt. Rub in the butter until the mixture is the consistency of fine bread crumbs. Add the water and mix to a firm dough. Divide the dough in quarters. Roll one quarter directly onto the buttered bottom of a 9-inch (23-cm) spring form pan. Bake in a 400°F (200°C) oven for about ten minutes or until golden brown.
2. Roll out the other three quarters to fit the sides of the spring form pan. Press the edges together and trim the top even. Reassemble the pan and set aside.
3. Mix the cream cheese with the sugar until soft and smooth.
4. Add the eggs one at a time, beating well after each addition. Mix in the vanilla.
5. Pour the cheese mixture into the prepared pastry and bake in a 350°F (180°C) oven for about 20 minutes. Turn the heat off and leave the cake in the oven to cool. When cool, chill for two hours.
6. In a saucepan mix together the sultana raisins, sugar, milk, lemon rind and vanilla. Cook over a low heat, stirring frequently, until thickened. Cool, then spread over the chilled cheesecake.
7. Mix together the plain flour, butter and brown sugar. Sprinkle over the cheesecake and quickly brown in a hot oven.

Serves 8-10.

Cherry Cheesecake

Crust:
1½ cups crushed graham crackers
1½ tablespoons sugar
1½ teaspoons cinnamon
½ cup (125 ml) melted butter

Filling:
½ lb (250 g) cream cheese
½ cup sugar
2 eggs, separated
1½ tablespoons plain flour
⅛ teaspoon salt

½ teaspoon vanilla essence
1½ teaspoons grated lemon rind
½ cup (125 ml) evaporated milk, chilled
1¼ tablespoons lemon juice

Topping:
1½ cups stoned cherries or 1 can (425 g) cherries
1 teaspoon gelatin
2 drops red coloring

1. Mix together the graham cracker crumbs, sugar, cinnamon and melted butter. Press on the bottom and sides of a 9-inch (23-cm) spring form pan. Chill.
2. Cream the cream cheese until softened.
3. Add sugar, egg yolks (one at a time), flour, salt, vanilla essence and lemon rind. Mix thoroughly.
4. Beat the evaporated milk until thick, then add the lemon juice and continue beating until stiff. Gently fold into the cheese mixture.
5. Beat the egg whites until stiff and fold into the cheese mixture. Pour into the prepared crust.
6. Bake in a 325°F (160°C) oven for about one hour. Leave in the oven until cool. Chill.
7. If fresh cherries are used, put into a saucepan with enough water to cover and ½ cup sugar. Mix well and bring to a boil. Reduce heat and simmer for about ten minutes. Drain reserving ¾ cup of the liquid. If canned cherries are used, drain and reserve ¾ cup of the syrup.
8. Arrange cherries on the top of the cheesecake.
9. Soak the gelatin in the reserved liquid for five minutes. Heat gently to dissolve the gelatin. Add the artificial coloring and chill until thickened. Spread over the cherries and chill until ready to serve.

Serves 8.

Superb Cream Cheesecake

Crust:
2½ cups crushed graham crackers
⅔ cup (165 ml) melted butter
1½ tablespoons sugar
1 teaspoon cinnamon

Filling:
1 lb (500 g) cream cheese
1 cup sugar
¼ cup plain flour

5 eggs, separated
2½ tablespoons lemon juice
grated rind of one lemon
2 cups (500 g) sour cream

Topping:
1 cup strawberries
1 cup (250 ml) apple juice
½ cup sugar
2 tablespoons cornstarch
2 tablespoons water

1. Mix the crushed graham crackers with the melted butter, sugar and cinnamon. Press on the bottom and sides of a 10-inch (25-cm) spring form pan. Refrigerate until ready to use.
2. Beat the cheese with the sugar until light.
3. Add the flour and egg yolks and beat until smooth.
4. Add the lemon juice, lemon rind and sour cream and beat with an electric mixer for ten minutes.
5. Beat the egg whites until stiff. Gently fold into the cheese mixture.
6. Pour into the prepared crust and bake in a 350°F (180°C) for one hour. Turn off the heat and leave in the oven for another hour. Open the oven door and leave for one more hour. (This slow cooling is very necessary to keep the cake from falling.) Remove from the oven and cool. Remove the sides of the pan.
7. Mix together the strawberries (or any other berry), apple juice and sugar in a saucepan and bring to a boil.
8. Mix the cornstarch with the water and add to the fruit. Cook, stirring constantly, until the topping is thick and transparent. Cool and spread on top of the cake.

Serves 8-10.

Orange Lemon Cheesecake

Crust:
1½ cups crushed corn flakes
3 tablespoons sugar
⅓ cup (85 g) butter
1 teaspoon grated lemon rind
1 teaspoon grated orange rind

Filling:
½ lb (250 g) cream cheese
1 pack lemon gelatin

2 cups (500 ml) very hot water
1 cup (250 ml) cream
2½ tablespoons sugar
1 cup chopped orange segments
1½ teaspoons grated lemon rind
orange segments

1. Mix together the crushed corn flakes, sugar, butter, lemon and orange rinds. Press on the bottom and sides of a shallow pie tin. Bake in a 350°F (180°C) oven for ten minutes. Remove from oven and cool.
2. Soften the cream cheese.
3. Mix together the lemon gelatin and the hot water. Stir until dissoved. Cool.
4. Stir the cooled gelatin mixture gradually into the cream cheese.
5. Beat together the cream and sugar until stiff. Fold into the cheese mixture.
6. Mix in the chopped orange segments. Pour into the prepared pie shell.
7. Sprinkle on the grated lemon rind and arrange orange segments on top.

Serves 8.

Tuscan Cheesecake

¾ lb (375 g) ricotta cheese
½ cup ground almonds
¼ cup orange peel
½ cup sugar
3 tablespoons raisins

2 tablespoons sultana raisins
4 egg yolks
grated rind of one lemon
sugar

1. Sieve the ricotta cheese through a fine strainer.
2. Mix with the almonds, orange peel, sugar, raisins and sultana raisins.
3. Beat the egg yolks until light yellow and add to the cheese mixture with the lemon rind.
4. Pour into a buttered mold and bake in a 350°F (180°C) oven for ½ hour. Sprinkle with sugar when cooked. (This cake does not have to be cooked. It is delicious served as a very thick cream.)

Serves 4.

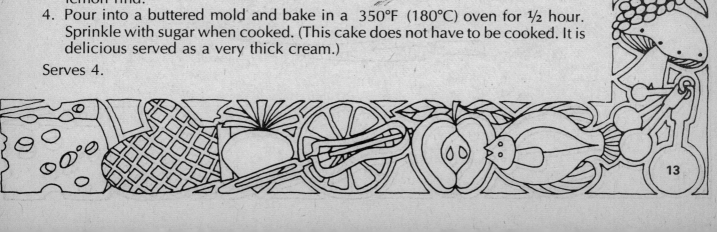

Jellied Cheesecake

Crust:
6 oz (185 g) graham crackers
3 tablespoons sugar
½ cup (125 ml) melted butter

Filling:
2½ tablespoons gelatin
¼ cup (65 ml) water
1½ cups crushed pineapple
milk
¼ cup (65 ml) milk

2½ tablespoons custard
  powder
1 lb (500 g) cottage cheese
2 egg whites
¼ cup sugar
1 cup (250 ml) cream
sweetened whipped cream
  to garnish
chopped crystallised ginger

1. Make the crust by crushing the graham crackers and mixing with the sugar and the melted butter. Press ¾ of the mixture on the bottom and sides of a 9-inch (23-cm) spring form pan. Set aside the remaining crust mixture.
2. Mix the gelatin and the water and allow to soak for five minutes.
3. Drain the pineapple and add enough milk to the pineapple liquid to make two cups. Put into a saucepan and heat.
4. Add the gelatin and mix until the gelatin is dissolved.
5. Mix the custard powder with the ¼ cup of milk and add to the saucepan. Stir constantly until thick.
6. Stir in the cheese and pineapple. Cool.
7. Beat the egg whites until almost stiff. Beat in the sugar.
8. Whip one cup of cream and fold into cheese mixture with beaten egg whites.
9. Pour into the crust and sprinkle the remaining crust mixture on top. Refrigerate until firm.
10. Serve garnished with sweetened whipped cream and ginger.

Serves 8.

Chocolate Cheesecake

Crust:
1½ cups chocolate cookie
  crumbs
½ cup (125 ml) melted butter
pinch of nutmeg

Filling:
2½ tablespoons gelatin

¾ cup sugar
1 cup (250 ml) milk
1 cup (250 ml) cream
2 eggs, separated
¼ lb (125 g) unsweetened
  chocolate
1 lb (500 g) cream cheese

CONTINUED ON NEXT PAGE

1. Mix together the cookie crumbs, melted butter and nutmeg. Press on the bottom and sides of a 9-inch (23-cm) spring form pan. Chill until ready to use.
2. Combine the gelatin and half the sugar in the top of a double boiler. Slowly add the milk and heat over simmering water until the gelatin is dissolved.
3. Add the cream and the egg yolks and mix thoroughly.
4. Add the chocolate and cook, stirring constantly until the chocolate is melted. Remove from heat and cool.
5. Cream the cream cheese until smooth and soft. Gradually add the chocolate mixture, beating constantly.
6. Beat the egg whites until stiff. Add the remaining sugar and beat until very stiff. Gently fold into the chocolate mixture.
7. Pour into the prepared crust and chill until firm.

Serves 8-10.

Restaurant Cheesecake

Crust:
2 cups crushed graham crackers
½ cup (125 ml) melted butter
2½ tablespoons brown sugar
1 teaspoon cinnamon

Filling:
1½ lb (750 g) cream cheese

1 cup sugar
2 tablespoons lemon juice
1½ teaspoons vanilla essence
3 eggs
whipped cream
nutmeg

1. Mix together the crushed graham crackers, melted butter, brown sugar and cinnamon. Firmly press on the bottom and sides of a 9-inch (23-cm) spring form pan. Put in the refrigerator until ready to use.
2. Mix the cream cheese with the sugar until smooth and soft.
3. Add the lemon juice, vanilla essence, and eggs. Mix well.
4. Pour into the prepared crust and bake in a 325°F (160°C) for about 45 minutes. Turn off the heat and leave in the oven until cool.
5. Serve topped with whipped cream and sprinkled with nutmeg.

Serves 10.

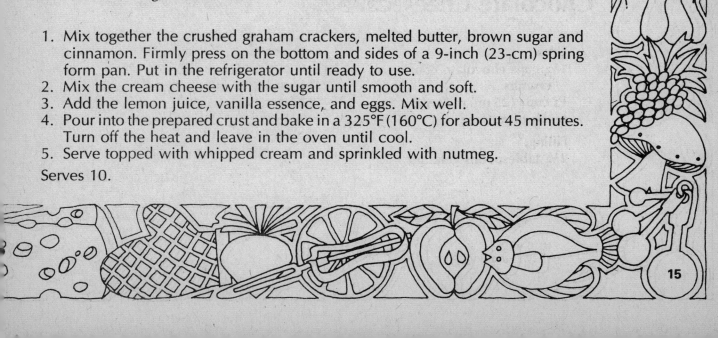

Pineapple Cottage Cheesecake

Crust:
2 cups finely crushed corn flakes
½ cup (125 ml) melted butter
5 tablespoons sugar
1 tablespoon cinnamon

Filling:
2½ tablespoons gelatin
4 tablespoons cold water
3 eggs, separated
½ cup sugar
⅛ teaspoon salt
1 cup (250 ml) milk
1 lb (500 g) cottage cheese
2 tablespoons lemon juice
grated rind of ½ lemon
½ cup crushed pineapple
⅓ cup (50 g) chopped glace cherries
1 teaspoon vanilla essence
½ cup (125 ml) cream

1. Make the crust by mixing together the crushed corn flakes, melted butter, sugar and cinnamon. Press on the bottom and sides of a 10-inch (25-cm) spring form pan.
2. Soak the gelatin in the water for five minutes.
3. Beat the egg yolks with the sugar and salt in the top of a double boiler.
4. Add the milk and cook over simmering water until thick and creamy, stirring constantly.
5. Add the gelatin and stir until dissolved.
6. Mix in the cheese, lemon juice, lemon rind, pineapple, cherries and vanilla essence. Remove from heat.
7. Beat the egg whites until stiff and whip the cream. Gently fold into the cheese mixture.
8. Pour into the crust and chill for several hours.

Serves 8-10.

Pineapple Cheesecake

Pastry:
1 cup plain flour
¼ cup sugar
⅓ cup (85 g) butter
1 egg yolk
½ teaspoon vanilla essence

Filling:
2 lb (1 kg) cream cheese
1½ cups sugar
4 tablespoons plain flour
1 teaspoon vanilla essence

4 eggs
2 egg yolks
¼ cup (65 ml) cream

Glaze:
4 tablespoons sugar
1¼ tablespoons cornstarch
1 can (425 g) crushed
   pineapple

glace cherries to garnish

1. Combine the flour and sugar in a mixing bowl.
2. Add the butter and mix until the mixture is the consistency of fine bread crumbs.
3. Add the egg yolks and vanilla essence and mix until the pastry just holds together. Chill.
4. Divide the pastry into thirds. Roll out one third to cover the bottom of a 10-inch (25-cm) spring form pan. Bake the bottom in a 400°F (200°C) oven until golden brown. Cool.
5. Roll out the other two thirds and line the sides of the spring form pan. Press edges together. Reassemble the pan. Chill.
6. Cream the cream cheese until soft. Add the sugar, flour and vanilla essence and beat well.
7. Add eggs and egg yolks beating well after each addition.
8. Stir in the cream and pour the mixture into the prepared pastry.
9. Bake in a 450°F (230°C) oven for ten minutes. Reduce heat to 350°F (180°C) and bake for another 1½ hours. Turn off heat and leave cake in the oven for another hour. Open the door of the oven and leave for another ½ hour. Remove from oven and cool. Remove the side of the spring form pan.
10. Make the glaze by mixing together the sugar and cornstarch in a small saucepan. Stir in the pineapple and cook, stirring constantly, over a medium heat until the mixture thickens. Cool and spread on top of the cake. Garnish with glace cherries.

Serves 10.

Apricot Cheese Pie

Crust:
1½ cups crushed vanilla
   wafers
⅓ cup (85 ml) melted butter
1 teaspoon cinnamon

Filling:
1 can (425 g) apricots

1 pack lemon gelatin
1¼ tablespoon lemon juice
1 teaspoon grated lemon rind
½ lb (250 g) cream cheese
whipped cream
crushed nuts
nutmeg

1. Mix together the crushed biscuits, melted butter and cinnamon. Press firmly on the bottom and sides of a 9-inch (23-cm) pie tin. Chill in refrigerator until ready to use.
2. Drain the apricots and reserve the liquid.
3. Add enough water to the liquid to make up to 1½ cups (375 ml). Add the lemon gelatin and heat until the gelatin is dissolved.
4. Add the lemon juice and lemon rind and chill until thickening.
5. Soften the cream cheese and mix with the gelatin mixture.
6. Chop the apricots and stir into the cheese mixture.
7. Pour into the prepared crust and chill until firm.
8. Serve with whipped cream, crushed nuts and a little nutmeg sprinkled on top.

Serves 6-8.

Coffee Cake with Cheese Filling

Cake:
3½ cups plain flour
2 tablespoons dry yeast
¾ cup (185 g) sour cream
½ cup (125 g) butter
¼ cup (65 ml) water
½ cup sugar
½ teaspoon salt
1½ teaspoons grated lemon rind
2 eggs

Cheese filling:
½ lb (250 g) cream cheese
¼ cup sugar
1 egg yolk
1 tablespoon sour cream
½ teaspoon vanilla essence
½ cup (80 g) raisins
½ cup (60 g) chopped walnuts

1 egg white
1¼ tablespoons sugar
¼ cup (60 g) chopped nuts

1. Sift 1½ cups of the flour and mix with the yeast in a large bowl.
2. In a saucepan mix together the sour cream, butter, water, sugar, salt and lemon rind. Heat until warm, stirring constantly.
3. Stir the sour cream mixture into the flour and yeast and beat for four minutes.
4. Stir in the remaining flour and mix to a soft dough.
5. Knead on a lightly floured board for five minutes. Put into an oiled bowl, cover and place in a warm spot until doubled in size (about 1½ hours).
6. Make the cheese filling by combining all the filling ingredients and mixing well.
7. Knead the dough a few times then roll out to a rectangle measuring 18 × 16 inch (45 × 40 cm).
8. Spread the cheese filling evenly over the dough and roll up. Cut the roll into two pieces to make it easier to handle. Place on a buttered baking tray, seam side down. Make cuts in the top of the rolls about 2 inches (5 cm) apart. Set aside in a warm place for 45 minutes or until it again doubles in size.
9. Brush with egg white and sprinkle with sugar and chopped nuts.
10. Bake in a 350°F (180°C) oven for about ½ hour or until golden brown. Remove from oven and serve warm.

Serves 8.

New York Cheesecake

Pastry:
1 cup plain flour
¼ cup sugar
1½ teaspoons grated lemon rind
½ teaspoon vanilla essence
1 egg yolk
¼ cup (65 g) butter

Filling:
2 lb (1 kg) cream cheese
1½ cups sugar

4 tablespoons plain flour
2 teaspoons grated orange rind
1½ teaspoons grated lemon rind
¼ teaspoon vanilla essence
4 eggs
2 egg yolks
½ cup (125 ml) cream
nutmeg

1. Mix together the flour, sugar, lemon rind and vanilla in a bowl. Add the egg yolk and butter and blend until the mixture forms a ball. Put into a plastic bag or wrap in wax paper and chill for about one hour.
2. Divide the dough into quarters. Butter a 9-inch (23-cm) spring form pan. Separate the bottom from the sides. Roll one quarter of the dough directly on the bottom of the pan. Trim the edges. Bake in a 400°F (200°C) oven for about ten minutes or until golden brown. Cool.
3. Roll out the remaining quarters and fit on the sides of the pan pressing the edges together. Trim the top edge. Chill in the refrigerator.
4. Mix together the cheese, sugar, flour, orange and lemon rind and vanilla essence.
5. Add the egg yolks and eggs one at a time, blending well after each addition.
6. Stir in the cream.
7. Put the spring form pan together and pour in the filling.
8. Bake in a 550°F (290°C) oven for ten minutes. Reduce the heat to 200°F (100°C) and bake for another hour. Remove from the oven and cool at room temperature. Sprinkle with nutmeg before serving.

Serves 10.

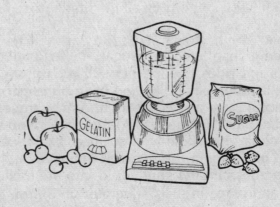

Velvet Cheesecake

Crust:
1½ cups crushed plain
  cookies
2½ tablespoons sugar
1 teaspoon cinnamon
⅓ cup (85 ml) melted butter

Filling:
1 lb (500 g) cream cheese

3 eggs, separated
⅔ cup honey
¼ cup custard powder
½ cup (125 ml) cream
1½ teaspoons cinnamon
whipped cream
crumbled honeycomb

1. Mix crushed cookies, sugar, cinnamon and melted butter. Press on the bottom and sides of a 9-inch (23-cm) spring form pan. Chill until ready to use.
2. Soften the cream cheese and beat in the egg yolks, honey and custard powder.
3. Beat the cream until thick and gently fold into the cream cheese mixture.
4. Beat the egg whites until stiff and fold into the cream cheese mixture.
5. Pour into the prepared crust and bake in a 325°F (160°C) oven for about one hour. Leave in the oven until cool.
6. Serve with whipped cream and honeycomb sprinkled on top. Serves 8.

Refrigerator Cheesecake

Crust:
2 cups crushed graham
  crackers
4 tablespoons sugar
½ cup (125 ml) melted butter
1 teaspoon cinnamon

Filling:
1 cup sugar

⅛ teaspoon salt
3 eggs, separated
½ cup (125 ml) lemon juice
4 tablespoons cornstarch
1 lb (500 g) cottage cheese
grated rind of one lemon
½ teaspoon vanilla essence

1. Mix together crushed graham crackers, sugar, melted butter and cinnamon. Press on the bottom and sides of a 10-inch (25-cm) spring form pan.
2. Combine the sugar, salt and egg yolks and beat until light.
3. Mix together the lemon juice and cornstarch. Add to the egg mixture.
4. Add the cheese and cook in the top of a double boiler over simmering water until thick, stirring constantly. Remove from heat and cool.
5. Add the lemon rind and vanilla essence and mix well.
6. Beat the egg whites until stiff and gently fold into the mixture.
7. Pour into the crust and place in the refrigerator until firm. Serves 8-10.

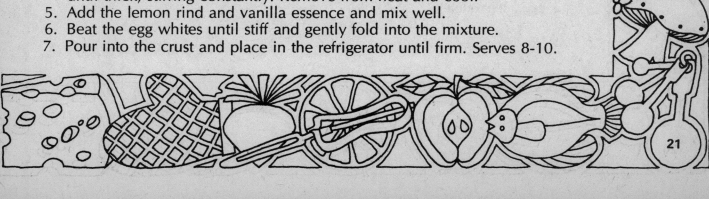

Nutty Crust Lemon Cheesecake

Crust:
1½ cups crushed graham
   crackers
2½ tablespoons sugar
2 teaspoons grated lemon
   rind
⅔ cup (80 g) finely chopped
   walnuts
⅔ cup (165 ml) melted butter

Filling:
¾ lb (375 g) cream cheese

⅔ cup (165 ml) sweetened
   condensed milk
4 tablespoons lemon juice
2 teaspoons grated lemon
   rind
⅔ cup (165 ml) cream

Topping:
3 tablespoons (45 g) butter
⅔ cup sugar
1 egg
2½ tablespoons lemon juice

1. Mix together the crushed graham crackers, sugar, lemon rind, walnuts and melted butter. Firmly press on the bottom and sides of a 9-inch (23-cm) spring form pan.
2. Soften the cream cheese, then beat together with the condensed milk, lemon juice and lemon rind until smooth.
3. Beat the cream and gently fold into the cream cheese mixture.
4. Pour into the prepared crust and chill.
5. Melt the butter in the top of a double boiler over simmering water. Remove from heat.
6. Mix in the sugar, lightly beaten egg and lemon juice.
7. Return to the heat and cook, stirring constantly, until the mixture thickens. Remove from heat and cool.
8. Spread the topping over the cheese cake and chill again before serving.

Serves 6-8.

Sour Cream Cheesecake

Crust:
1½ cups crushed graham
   crackers
4 tablespoons sugar
1½ teaspoons cinnamon
½ cup (125 ml) melted butter

Filling:
1 lb (500 g) cream cheese
2 eggs, separated

2 tablespoons cake
   flour
2 teaspoons grated lemon
   rind
½ cup (125 g) sour cream
½ cup (125 ml) milk
½ cup sugar
nutmeg

CONTINUED ON NEXT PAGE

CONTINUED FROM PREVIOUS PAGE

1. Mix together the crushed graham crackers, sugar, cinnamon and melted butter. Firmly press on the bottom and sides of a 9-inch (23-cm) spring form pan.
2. Soften the cream cheese and beat in the egg yolks, flour, lemon rind, sour cream and milk.
3. Beat the egg whites until stiff. Add the sugar and continue beating until the sugar dissolves. Fold into the cream cheese mixture.
4. Pour into the prepared crust and bake in a 325°F (160°C) oven for about one hour.
5. Serve chilled sprinkled with nutmeg.

Serves 8.

Tangerine Cheesecake

Crust:
2 cups crushed graham crackers
2½ tablespoons sugar
1 teaspoon cinnamon
½ cup (125 ml) melted butter

Filling:
1¼ tablespoons gelatin
¼ cup (65 ml) water

1 lb (500 g) cream cheese
⅔ cup sugar
1½ teaspoons vanilla essence
grated rind of one lemon
4 tablespoons lemon juice
1 can (310 g) tangerine segments
3 egg whites

1. Mix together the crushed graham crackers, sugar, cinnamon and melted butter. Press firmly on the bottom and sides of a 9-inch (23-cm) spring form pan. Chill until ready to use.
2. Mix the gelatin with the water and allow to soak for five minutes. Place over hot water and stir until dissolved.
3. Soften the cream cheese and beat in the sugar, vanilla essence and lemon rind.
4. Mix the lemon juice with enough of the liquid from the drained tangerines to make up ½ cup of liquid. Add this liquid to the cream cheese mixture with the dissolved gelatin.
5. Beat the egg whites until stiff and fold into the cream cheese mixture with the tangerine segments.
6. Pour into the prepared crust and chill until firm.

Serves 8.

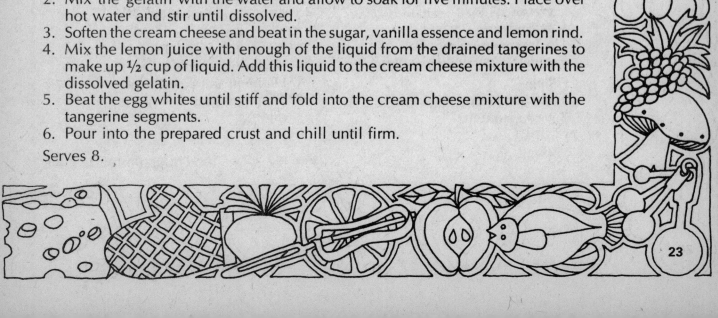

Raspberry Swirl Cheesecake

Crust:
1 cup graham crackers crumbs
¼ cup (65 ml) melted butter
1 teaspoon cinnamon

Filling:
1 cup sugar
⅓ cup (85 ml) water
⅛ teaspoon baking powder

3 egg whites
1 lb (500 g) cream cheese
½ cup (125 g) sour cream
2 teaspoons vanilla essence
1¼ tablespoons grated lemon rind
1 can (425 g) raspberries
½ cup (125 ml) cream, whipped

1. Mix together the graham cracker crumbs, melted butter and cinnamon. Press on the bottom and sides of a 9-inch (23-cm) spring form pan. Put in refrigerator until ready to use.
2. Mix together the sugar, water and baking powder in a small saucepan. Bring to a boil and continue to boil for eight minutes. Remove from heat.
3. Beat the egg whites until stiff. Pour on the sugar syrup and continue beating until the egg whites are very stiff and the mixture cools.
4. Cream the cream cheese and mix in the sour cream, vanilla essence and lemon rind.
5. Add the egg white mixture a little at a time until it is all thoroughly blended.
6. Pour layers of the cheese mixture and the raspberries into the prepared crust. Spread whipped cream on top.

Serves 10.

California Cheesecake

Crust:
2 cups crushed graham crackers
¼ cup sugar
1 teaspoon cinnamon
½ cup (125 ml) melted butter

Filling:
750 g (1½ lb) cream cheese
1 cup sugar

4 eggs, beaten
1 tablespoon lemon juice
⅛ teaspoon salt
2½ cups (625 g) sour cream
4 tablespoons sugar
1 teaspoon vanilla essence
2 teaspoons grated lemon rind

CONTINUED ON NEXT PAGE

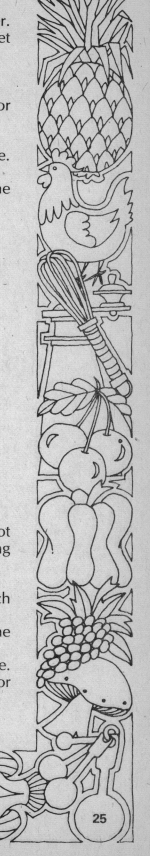

CONTINUED FROM PREVIOUS PAGE

1. Mix the graham cracker crumbs with the sugar, cinnamon and melted butter. Press over the bottom and sides of a 10-inch (25-cm) spring form pan. Set aside.
2. Cream the cheese.
3. Beat the eggs with the one cup of sugar until thick and light yellow colored.
4. Add to the cheese with the lemon juice and salt. Beat well with a rotary or electric beater.
5. Pour into the crust and bake in a 375°F (190°C) oven for 25 minutes.
6. Mix the sour cream with the five tablespoons sugar and the vanilla essence. Spread over cake and bake at 475°F (250°C) oven for ten minutes.
7. When cool, place in the refrigerator for several hours. Remove from the refrigerator about an hour before serving.

Serves 8-10.

Nutty Cheesecake

Crust:
2 cups crushed graham
  crackers
¼ cup (30 g) crushed nuts
½ cup (125 ml) melted butter
1¼ tablespoons hot water
pinch of nutmeg

Filling:
½ lb (250 g) cream cheese
½ cup sugar

1½ teaspoons vanilla
  essence
3 eggs, beaten

Topping:
1 cup (250 g) sour cream
½ teaspoon vanilla essence
2 tablespoons sugar
2½ tablespoons chopped
  nuts

1. Mix together the crushed graham crackers, crushed nuts, melted butter, hot water and nutmeg. Press on the bottom and sides of a 8-inch (20-cm) spring form pan. Chill.
2. Beat together the cream cheese and sugar until smooth and soft.
3. Add the vanilla essence and the eggs, one at a time, beating well after each addition. Pour into the prepared crust.
4. Bake in a 350°F (180°C) oven for about 45 minutes. Remove the cake from the oven but do not turn the heat off.
5. Blend together the sour cream, sugar and vanilla and spread over the cake. Sprinkle on the chopped nuts and return to the oven for about ten minutes or until the topping is set. Cool and refrigerate for several hours before serving.

Serves 8-10.

Creme de Menthe Cheesecake

Crust:
1½ cups crushed graham
   crackers
1 teaspoon cinnamon
⅓ cup (85 ml) melted butter

Filling:
3 oz (90 g) dark chocolate
3 eggs
⅔ cup sugar

½ lb (250 g) cream cheese
1 cup (250 ml) cream
2½ tablespoons creme de
   menthe
5 tablespoons plain flour
⅛ teaspoon baking soda
⅛ teaspoon salt
whipped cream
grated chocolate

1. Mix together the crushed graham crackers, cinnamon and melted butter. Firmly press on the bottom and sides of a 8-inch (20-cm) spring form pan. Chill until ready to use.
2. Melt the chocolate in a small bowl over hot water.
3. Beat together the eggs and sugar until thick and light yellow colored.
4. Soften the cream cheese and beat with the cream until smooth.
5. Add the melted chocolate to the cream cheese mixture and stir until well blended.
6. Add the egg mixture to the chocolate mixture with the creme de menthe. Mix gently but thoroughly.
7. Sift together the flour, baking soda and salt and mix into the chocolate mixture.
8. Pour into the prepared crust and bake in a 300°F (150°C) oven for about one hour. Turn off the heat and allow the cake to cool in the oven with the door open.
9. Serve topped with whipped cream and grated chocolate.

Serves 8.

Quick Sherry Cheesecake

Crust:
1½ cups crushed graham
   crackers
2½ tablespoons sugar
1 teaspoon cinnamon
½ cup (125 ml) melted butter

Filling:
1 lb (500 g) cream cheese
½ cup sugar
3 eggs
5 tablespoons sherry
2 teaspoons lemon juice

CONTINUED ON NEXT PAGE

1. Mix together the crushed crackers, sugar, cinnamon and melted butter. Press on the bottom of a 9-inch (23-cm) spring form pan. Chill until ready to use.
2. Soften the cream cheese, then beat in the sugar until the mixture is smooth.
3. Add the eggs one at a time, beating well after each addition.
4. Add the sherry and lemon juice and mix thoroughly.
5. Pour into the prepared crust and bake in a 300°F (150°C) oven for about one hour. Turn off the heat and leave the cheesecake in the oven with the door open until cool.
6. Top with whipped cream, sprinkle with nutmeg and serve. Serves 8.

Apricot Cheesecake

Crust:
1½ cups crushed graham
   crackers
2½ tablespoons sugar
1 teaspoon cinnamon
⅓ cup (85 ml) melted butter

Filling:
1 lb (500 g) cream cheese
1 cup sugar
4 eggs, separated
½ cup plain flour

1 cup (250 ml) cream
1½ teaspoons grated lemon
   rind
2 tablespoons lemon
   juice
¾ teaspoon vanilla essence
½ cup (65 g) chopped dried
   apricots
½ cup sugar
1¼ cups (300 ml) water

1. Mix together the crushed graham crackers, sugar, cinnamon and melted butter. Firmly press on the bottom and sides of a 9-inch (23-cm) spring form pan.
2. Soften the cream cheese and beat in the sugar until smooth.
3. Add the egg yolks one at a time, beating well after each addition.
4. Add the flour and mix well.
5. Whip the cream and gently fold in with the lemon rind, lemon juice and vanilla.
6. Beat the egg whites until stiff and fold into the cream cheese mixture.
7. Soak the apricots in the water for ½ hour. Add sugar and simmer until tender. Sieve through a fine strainer. Cool.
8. Pour half the cream cheese mixture into the prepared crust. Spoon the apricot puree over it, then pour on the other half of the cheese mixture. Mix with a knife a few times to create a marble pattern.
9. Bake in a 325°F (160°C) oven for about one hour. Turn off heat and leave in the oven for another hour, then chill in the refrigerator. Serves 8-10.

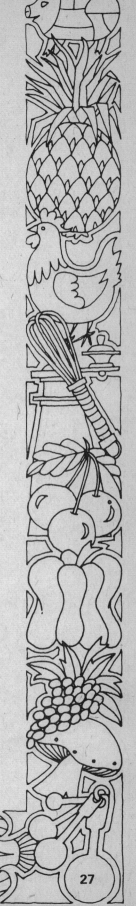

Caramel Cheesecake

Crust:
1½ cups crushed graham
    crackers
1 teaspoon cinnamon
1½ tablespoons sugar
½ cup (125 ml) melted butter

Filling:
1¼ tablespoons gelatin
¼ cup (65 ml) water
½ lb (250 g) cream cheese
¼ cup sugar

2 egg yolks
4 tablespoons lemon juice

Topping:
2 teaspoons gelatin
¼ cup (65 ml) water
3 tablespoons (45 g) butter
3 tablespoons brown sugar
2½ tablespoons sweetened
    condensed milk
1½ tablespoons maple syrup
⅓ cup (85 ml) hot water

1. Mix crushed crackers, cinnamon, sugar and melted butter. Press on the bottom of a 8-inch (20-cm) spring form pan. Chill until ready to use.
2. Blend the gelatin with the water and allow to soak for five minutes. Place over hot water and stir until dissolved.
3. Soften the cream cheese, then beat with the sugar until smooth.
4. Mix in the egg yolks, lemon juice and gelatin. Pour into the prepared crust and chill until set.
5. Mix the two teaspoons of gelatin with the water and soak for five minutes.
6. Mix together the brown sugar, condensed milk and maple syrup in a small saucepan. Cook over a medium heat, stirring constantly until the mixture leaves the sides of the pan.
7. Remove from the heat and slowly pour in the hot water, stirring constantly. Return to the heat and stir in the gelatin until dissolved. Cool.
8. Pour the caramel topping over the filling and chill until set. Serves 8.

Viennese Cheesecake

Crust:
1 cup crushed graham
    crackers
1 teaspoon cinnamon
2½ tablespoons sugar
⅓ cup (85 ml) melted butter

Filling:
1 lb (500 g) cream cheese
2 eggs

½ cup sugar
2 tablespoons lemon
    juice
1 teaspoon grated lemon
    rind
1½ cups (375 g) sour cream
1 teaspoon vanilla essence
blanched almonds

CONTINUED ON NEXT PAGE

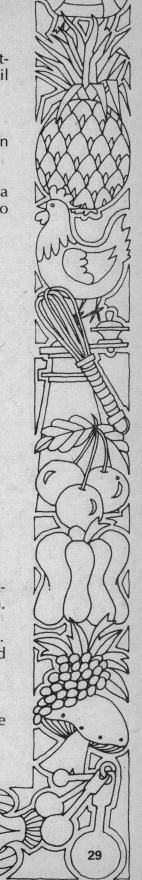

CONTINUED FROM PREVIOUS PAGE

1. Mix together the crushed graham crackers, cinnamon, sugar and melted butter. Press firmly on the bottom of a 9-inch (23-cm) spring form pan. Chill until ready to use.
2. Beat the cream cheese until soft and smooth.
3. Mix together the eggs and half the sugar until thick.
4. Add the softened cream cheese to the egg and sugar mixture with the lemon juice and lemon rind. Mix well.
5. Pour into the prepared crust and bake in a 350°F (180°C) oven for ½ hour.
6. Meanwhile mix together the remaining sugar with the sour cream and vanilla essence. Spoon over the cake and decorate with blanched almonds. Return to the oven and bake for another ten minutes.

Serves 6-8.

Chocolate Cottage Cheesecake

Crust:
1½ cups crushed graham
   crackers
1¼ tablespoons sugar
1 teaspoon cinnamon
⅓ cup (85 ml) melted butter

Filling:
1½ lb (750 g) cottage
   cheese

4 egg whites
1 cup sugar
⅔ cup (165 ml) cream
2 oz (60 g) dark chocolate

1. Mix together the crushed graham crackers, sugar, cinnamon and melted butter. Firmly press on the bottom and sides of a 9-inch (23-cm) spring form pan. Chill until ready to use.
2. Press the cottage cheese through a strainer and beat until soft and creamy.
3. Beat the egg whites until they form soft peaks, then add the sugar slowly and continue beating until stiff.
4. Fold into the cottage cheese and pour into the prepared crust.
5. Bake in 350°F (180°C) oven for about ½ hour. Cool.
6. Whip the cream and beat in the melted chocolate. Spread over the top of the cake and refrigerate for an hour or so.

Serves 8.

Grapefruit Orange Cheesecake

Crust:
2 cups crushed coconut cookies
2 teaspoons grated lemon rind
½ cup (125 ml) melted butter

Filling:
2 grapefruit
3 oranges
3 eggs
⅔ cup sugar

⅛ teaspoon salt
½ cup (125 ml) orange juice
1¼ tablespoons gelatin
¼ cup (65 ml) water
1 lb (500 g) cream cheese
1¼ tablespoons lemon juice
2 teaspoons grated orange rind
1 teaspoon grated lemon rind
⅔ cup (165 ml) cream

1. Mix together the crushed cookies, lemon rind and melted butter. Firmly press on the bottom of a 9-inch (23-cm) spring form pan.
2. Peel the grapefruit and the oranges and cut the segments into small pieces.
3. Separate two eggs and combine the egg yolks, the remaining whole egg, sugar, salt and one tablespoon of orange juice in the top of a double boiler. Place over simmering water and cook, stirring constantly, until the mixture thickens. Remove from heat.
4. Soak the gelatin in the water for five minutes. Stir into the warm custard until dissolved.
5. Press the cream cheese through a strainer and beat with remaining orange juice, lemon juice and rinds until smooth. Beat into the custard.
6. Fold in the grapefruit and orange pieces.
7. Lightly whip the cream and beat the egg whites until they form soft peaks. Fold the cream and egg whites into the cheese mixture.
8. Pour into the prepared spring form pan and chill for several hours or overnight.

Lemon Refrigerator Cheesecake

Crust:
2 cups crushed plain vanilla cookies
½ cup (125 ml) melted butter
2½ tablespoons sugar
1½ teaspoons cinnamon

Filling:
1 pack lemon gelatin
¾ cup (185 ml) boiling water

2 tablespoons grated lemon rind
⅓ cup (85 ml) lemon juice
1 can (410 g) evaporated milk, chilled
½ lb (250 g) cream cheese
1 cup sugar
1½ teaspoons vanilla essence

CONTINUED ON NEXT PAGE

1. Mix crushed cookies, melted butter, sugar and cinnamon. Press on bottom and sides of a 9-inch (23-cm) spring form pan. Refrigerate until ready for use.
2. Mix together the gelatin, boiling water, lemon rind and lemon juice. Stir until the gelatin is dissolved. Cool slightly.
3. Beat the evaporated milk with a rotary or electric mixer until thick.
4. Beat cream cheese with sugar until soft and smooth. Add vanilla essence.
5. Add the beaten milk to the cheese mixture and fold in the gelatin mixture.
6. Pour into the prepared crust and chill for several hours before serving.

Serves 8.

Blender Mango Cheesecake

Crust:
1½ cups crushed graham crackers
½ cup desiccated coconut
1½ teaspoons cinnamon
2½ tablespoons sugar
⅔ cup (165 ml) melted butter

Filling:
2½ tablespoons gelatin
1¼ tablespoons grated lemon rind
2 tablespoons lemon juice

½ cup (125 ml) boiling water
½ cup sugar
3 egg yolks
¾ lb (375 g) cream cheese
1 lb (500 g) mashed mango pulp
½ cup (125 ml) cold water
1½ cups (375 g) sour cream
⅔ cup (165 ml) cream

1. Mix the crushed graham crackers, coconut, cinnamon, sugar and melted butter together. Firmly press on the bottom and sides of a 9-inch (23-cm) spring form pan. Chill until ready to use.
2. Put the gelatin, lemon rind, lemon juice and boiling water in an electric blender and whirl for about 30 seconds.
3. Add the sugar, egg yolks and softened cream cheese. Whirl on high speed for another 30 seconds.
4. Add the mango pulp (keep some aside for the top of the cake), cold water and sour cream. Blend until all the ingredients are well mixed.
5. Pour into the prepared crust and chill until firm.
6. Whip the cream and gently fold in the reserved mango pulp. Spread over the cake and serve.

Serves 8.

Pawpaw Cheesecake

Crust:
1½ cups crushed coconut
   cookies
2½ tablespoons sugar
1½ teaspoons cinnamon
½ teaspoon nutmeg
½ cup (125 ml) melted butter

Filling:
¾ lb (375 g) cream cheese
⅓ cup sugar
2 eggs, separated

2 teaspoons grated orange
   rind
2 teaspoons grated lemon
   rind
2½ tablespoons lemon juice
1½ cups chopped pawpaw
⅔ cup (165 ml) cream
¼ cup sugar
whipped cream
cinnamon

1. Mix crushed cookies, sugar, cinnamon, nutmeg and melted butter. Press on the sides of a 9-inch (23-cm) spring form pan. Chill until ready to use.
2. Soften cream cheese, then beat in ⅓ cup sugar until mixture is smooth.
3. Lightly beat the egg yolks and stir into the mixture until just blended.
4. Add the orange and lemon rind, lemon juice and chopped pawpaw.
5. Whip the cream and fold into the cheese mixture.
6. Beat the egg whites until they form soft peaks. Slowly add the sugar while continuing to beat until the sugar is dissolved and the egg whites are stiff. Fold into the cream cheese mixture.
7. Pour filling into the prepared crust and bake in a 350°F (180°C) oven for ten minutes. Reduce heat to 325°F (160°C) and bake for another ½ hour or until set. Turn off heat, open oven door and leave cake in the oven to cool.
8. Top with whipped cream and sprinkle with cinnamon before serving.

Serves 8.

Summer Cheesecake

Crust:
2 cups crushed graham
   crackers
4 tablespoons sugar
1½ teaspooons cinnamon
½ cup desiccated coconut
⅔ cup (165 ml) melted butter

Filling:
½ lb (250 g) cottage cheese

½ lb (250 g) cream cheese
⅔ cup sugar
1½ teaspoons vanilla essence
1¼ tablespoons gelatin
½ cup (125 ml) water
1½ cups (375 ml) cream
3 egg whites
1 cup halved seedless grapes
1 cup halved strawberries

CONTINUED ON NEXT PAGE

CONTINUED FROM PREVIOUS PAGE

1. Mix together the crushed graham crackers, sugar, cinnamon, coconut and melted butter. Firmly press on the bottom and sides of a 10-inch (25-cm) spring form pan. Chill until ready to use.
2. Press the cottage cheese and cream cheese through a strainer.
3. Beat the two cheeses together with the sugar and vanilla until smooth.
4. Soak the gelatin in the water for five minutes. Place over hot water and stir until dissolved.
5. Whip one cup of the cream and beat the egg whites until soft peaks form. Fold both the cream and the egg whites into the cheese mixture.
6. Pour into the prepared crust and chill.
7. Just before serving, whip the remaining cream and spread over the top of the cake. Arrange the grapes and strawberries in the cream.

Serves 10.

Nut Fruit Cake

¾ cup (185 g) butter
1½ cups sugar
½ lb (250 g) cream cheese
2 teaspoons vanilla essence
4 eggs
2 cups plain flour
1½ teaspoons baking powder
½ teaspoon salt
½ cup chopped dates

¼ cup raisins
¼ cup currants
1 cup finely chopped walnuts
1½ teaspoons grated orange rind
1½ cups confectioner's sugar
1½ tablespoons orange juice
2 teaspoons lemon juice

1. Cream together the butter and sugar until light and fluffy.
2. Soften the cream cheese and beat into the butter and sugar mixture with the vanilla essence.
3. Add the eggs one at a time, beating well after each addition.
4. Sift together the flour, baking powder and salt and gradually add to the mixture beating well.
5. Add the dates, raisins, currants, walnuts and orange rind.
6. Pour into a well-buttered and floured cake tin lined with wax paper and bake in a 350°F (180°C) oven for about 1½ hours. Cool slightly, then remove from tin and cool completely.
7. Mix together the orange juice, lemon juice and confectioner's sugar. Spread over the top of the cake.

Serves 8.

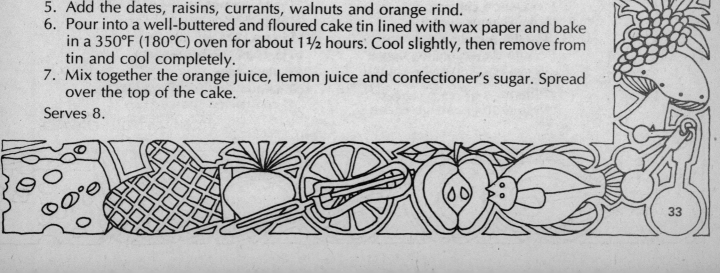

Citrus Cheesecake

Crust:
1½ cups crushed coconut
   cookies
2½ tablespoons sugar
½ cup (125 ml) melted butter

Filling:
1¼ tablespoons gelatin
¼ cup (65 ml) water
3 eggs, separated
¼ teaspoon salt
½ cup (125 ml) milk
½ cup sugar

½ cup brown sugar
4 tablespoons lemon juice
4 tablespoons orange juice
4 tablespoons grapefruit juice
1½ tablespoons grated lemon
   rind
1 lb (500 g) cream cheese
1½ teaspoons vanilla essence
1 cup (250 ml) cream
1½ tablespoons grated orange
   rind

1. Mix together the crushed cookies, sugar and melted butter. Press firmly on the bottom and sides of a 9-inch (23-cm) spring form pan. Chill until ready to use.
2. Soak the gelatin in the water for five minutes.
3. Mix the egg yolks with the salt and milk in the top of a double boiler. Place over simmering water and cook, stirring constantly, until thick. Remove from heat.
4. Add sugar, brown sugar and gelatin to the egg yolk mixture and stir until the sugars and the gelatin are dissolved.
5. Add the juices and grated lemon rind. Cool until the mixture begins to thicken.
6. Press the cream cheese through a strainer and beat with the vanilla essence and cooled gelatine mixture until smooth.
7. Whip the cream and fold into the cream cheese mixture.
8. Beat the egg whites until they form soft peaks and fold into the cheese mixture.
9. Pour into the prepared crust and sprinkle with grated orange rind. Chill for several hours or overnight. Serves 8.

Rich Cream Cheesecake

Crust:
2 cups crushed graham
   crackers
1 teaspoon cinnamon
¼ teaspoon nutmeg
2½ tablespoons sugar
⅔ cup (165 ml) melted butter

Filling:
1½ lb (750 g) cream cheese

1 cup sugar
2 tablespoons plain flour
⅛ teaspoon salt
5 eggs, separated
1 egg
1½ cups (375 g) sour cream
4 tablespoons lemon juice
¼ cup sugar
cinnamon

CONTINUED ON NEXT PAGE

34

CONTINUED FROM PREVIOUS PAGE

1. Mix together the crushed graham crackers, cinnamon, nutmeg, sugar and melted butter. Firmly press on the bottom and sides of a 10-inch (25-cm) spring form pan. Chill until ready to use.
2. Soften the cream cheese and beat in the cup of sugar.
3. Add the flour and salt and mix well.
4. Beat in the egg yolks plus the whole egg, sour cream and lemon juice.
5. Beat the egg whites until they form soft peaks, then add the sugar and beat until stiff. Fold into the cream cheese mixture.
6. Pour into the prepared crust and bake in a 300°F (150°C) oven for 1½ hours. Turn off the heat and let the cake cool in the oven. Chill in the refrigerator until firm. Serve sprinkled with cinnamon. Serves 10.

Sour Cream Topped Cheesecake

Crust:
1 cup cake flour
⅛ teaspoon salt
½ cup (125 g) butter
½ teaspoon vanilla essence
½ cup sugar
2 eggs
3 teaspoons milk

Filling:
½ lb (250 g) cream cheese
¾ cup sugar

½ cup (125 ml) cream
1 teaspoon vanilla
2 eggs

Topping:
1 cup (250 g) sour cream
2½ tablespoons sugar
1 teaspoon lemon juice
1¼ tablespoons milk
cinnamon

1. Sift together flour and salt. Set aside.
2. Cream together butter, vanilla and sugar until light and fluffy.
3. Stir in the eggs and milk and beat well.
4. Add flour and salt and blend well.
5. Butter a 9-inch (23-cm) spring form pan and lightly press crust on the bottom. Set aside.
6. Soften the cream cheese and beat in the sugar until smooth.
7. Stir in the cream and vanilla.
8. Lightly beat the eggs and thoroughly mix into the cream cheese mixture. Pour over prepared crust.
9. Bake in a 325°F (160°C) oven for one hour.
10. Mix together the sour cream, sugar, lemon juice and milk. Spread over the cake and bake for another ten minutes. Cool. Refrigerate for several hours.

Serves 8.

Cafe Au Lait Cheesecake

Crust:
1½ cups crushed plain
  vanilla cookies
½ cup crushed chocolate
  cookies
1 teaspoon cinnamon
⅔ cup (165 ml) melted butter

Filling:
1¼ tablespoons gelatin
¼ cup (65 ml) water

1 lb (500 g) cottage cheese
½ cup brown sugar
1¼ tablespoons instant coffee
  powder
1½ teaspoons vanilla essence
2 eggs, separated
½ cup (125 ml) cream
¼ cup sugar
whipped cream
nutmeg

1. Mix together the crushed cookies, cinnamon and melted butter. Firmly press on the bottom and sides of a 9-inch (23-cm) spring form pan. Chill until ready to use.
2. Soak the gelatin in the water for five minutes. Place over hot water and stir until dissolved.
3. Press the cottage cheese through a strainer, then beat in the brown sugar, instant coffee, vanilla essence, egg yolks, cream and gelatin.
4. Beat the egg whites until they form soft peaks. Slowly add the sugar while continuing to beat until stiff. Fold into the cheese mixture.
5. Pour into the prepared crust and chill until set.
6. Serve with whipped cream spread on top and sprinkled with nutmeg.

Serves 8.

Coffee Cream Cheesecake

Crust:
1½ cups crushed coconut
  cookies
½ cup desiccated coconut
½ teaspoon nutmeg
½ cup (125 ml) melted butter

Filling:
3 eggs, separated
1 cup (250 ml) milk
½ cup sugar
1¼ tablespoons gelatin
⅛ teaspoon salt

1¼ tablespoons instant coffee
  powder
1 lb (500 g) cream cheese
⅓ cup sugar
⅔ cup (165 ml) cream

Coffee Cream:
⅔ cup (165 ml) cream
1½ teaspoons instant coffee
  powder
1½ teaspoons sugar

CONTINUED ON NEXT PAGE

CONTINUED FROM PREVIOUS PAGE

1. Mix together the crushed cookies, coconut, nutmeg and melted butter. Firmly press on the bottom and sides of a 9-inch (23-cm) spring form pan. Chill until ready to use.
2. Lightly beat the egg yolks with the milk in a saucepan.
3. Mix in the sugar, gelatin and salt and heat until the sugar and gelatin are dissolved. Remove from heat.
4. Stir in the instant coffee powder and cool.
5. Press the cream cheese through a strainer and beat with the gelatin mixture until smooth.
6. Beat the egg whites until they form soft peaks. Slowly add the sugar and continue to beat until stiff. Fold into the cheese mixture.
7. Whip the cream and gently fold into the mixture.
8. Pour into the prepared crust and chill until firm.
9. Mix together the cream, instant coffee powder and sugar. Chill for at least 30 minutes, then beat until thick. Spread on the top of the cheesecake and serve.

Serves 8.

Australian Fruit Tart

Pastry:
1 cup plain flour
¼ cup sugar
grated rind of one lemon
1 egg yolk
½ cup (125 g) butter

Filling:
1 pack vanilla instant pudding
¼ lb (125 g) cream cheese, at room temperature

1 can (425 g) peach slices, drained
1 cup halved strawberries
½ lb (250 g) green grapes, halved and seeded
1 cup cut up orange segments
½ cup apricot jam

1. Mix together the flour and sugar. Add the lemon rind, egg yolk and butter. Mix well until the dough forms a ball. Roll out and line a 10-inch (25-cm) tart tin. Bake in a 400°F (200°C) oven until golden brown. Remove from oven and cool.
2. Prepare the vanilla pudding according to the directions on the pack.
3. Mix with the softened cream cheese. Pour into the pastry shell.
4. Arrange the fruit on the cheese mixture.
5. Heat the jam in a saucepan until melted and brush on the fruit. Chill.

Serves 6-8.

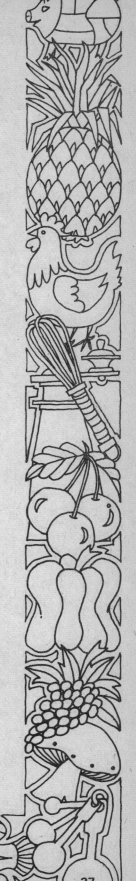

Sweet Ginger Rum Cheesecake

Crust:
2 cups crushed graham
crackers
1½ teaspoons ground ginger
½ cup (125 ml) melted butter

Filling:
1 lb (500 g) cream cheese
⅔ cup brown sugar
3 eggs, separated
2½ tablespoons rum
4 tablespoons chopped
crystallised ginger

1¼ tablespoons gelatin
¼ cup (65 ml) water
1 cup (250 ml) cream

Topping:
2 egg whites
2 tablespoons sugar
1½ cups (375 ml) cream
1½ tablespoons rum
2 tablespoons chopped
crystallised ginger

1. Mix crushed graham crackers, ground ginger and melted butter. Press on the bottom and sides of a 9-inch (23-cm) spring form pan. Chill until ready to use.
2. Soften the cream cheese, then beat in the brown sugar until smooth.
3. Beat in the egg yolks, rum and ginger.
4. Mix the gelatin with the water and allow to soak for five minutes. Place over hot water and stir until dissolved. Mix into the cream cheese mixture.
5. Beat the cream and fold into the mixture.
6. Beat the egg whites until stiff and fold into the mixture.
7. Pour into the prepared crust and chill.
8. Beat the two egg whites until they form soft peaks. Slowly add the sugar and continue to beat until stiff.
9. Beat the cream with the rum and fold into the egg whites with the ginger. Spread over the top of the cheesecake and chill well. Serves 8.

Easy Jello Cheesecake

Crust:
1½ cups crushed coconut
cookies
½ cup desiccated coconut
½ cup (125 ml) melted butter

Filling:
1 pack lemon jello
½ cup (125 ml) boiling water

½ cup (125 ml) lemon juice
2 teaspoons grated lemon
rind
1 teaspoon vanilla essence
1 can (440 g) sweetened
condensed milk
½ lb (250 g) cream cheese
grated lemon rind to decorate

CONTINUED ON NEXT PAGE

1. Mix together the crushed cookies, coconut and melted butter. Firmly press on the bottom and sides of a 9-inch (23-cm) spring form pan. Chill.
2. Mix the lemon jello with the boiling water and stir until dissolved.
3. Add the lemon juice and lemon rind and mix well. Cool.
4. Beat the condensed milk with the vanilla essence until thick.
5. Soften the cream cheese and combine with the jello mixture and the beaten condensed milk. Blend thoroughly.
6. Pour into the prepared crust, sprinkle with grated lemon rind and chill until firm.

Serves 6-8.

Quick Lemon Cheesecake

Crust:
1½ cups crushed plain vanilla cookies
1 teaspoon grated lemon rind
1 teaspoon cinnamon
½ cup (125 ml) melted butter

Filling:
1 lb (500 g) cream cheese
1 cup (250 ml) sweetened condensed milk
½ cup (125 ml) lemon juice
2 teaspoons grated lemon rind
1 cup (250 ml) cream
whipped cream
grated lemon rind
glace cherries

1. Mix crushed cookies, lemon rind, cinnamon and melted butter. Press on the bottom and sides of a 9-inch (23-cm) spring form pan. Chill until ready to use.
2. Soften the cream cheese, then beat together with the condensed milk, lemon juice and lemon rind.
3. Whip the cream and fold into the cream cheese mixture.
4. Pour into the prepared crust and chill for several hours or overnight.
5. Serve decorated with whipped cream, lemon rind and glace cherries.

Serves 8.

Cointreau Cheesecake

Crust:
2 cups crushed graham crackers
2 teaspoons grated orange rind
⅔ cup (165 ml) melted butter

Filling:
2 eggs, separated
⅔ cup sugar
1¼ tablespoons gelatin
¼ teaspoon salt

½ cup (125 ml) evaporated milk
1½ teaspoons grated orange rind
375 g (¾ lb) cream cheese
1¼ tablespoons lemon juice
½ teaspoon vanilla essence
4 tablespoons Cointreau
¼ cup sugar
⅔ cup (165 ml) cream

1. Mix together the crushed graham crackers, orange rind and melted butter. Firmly press on the bottom and sides of a 9-inch (23-cm) spring form pan. Chill until ready to use.
2. Combine the egg yolks, sugar, gelatin, salt and evaporated milk in the top of a double boiler. Place over simmering water and cook, stirring constantly, until the mixture thickens.
3. Stir in the grated orange rind and cool.
4. Press the cream cheese through a strainer and beat together with the lemon juice, vanilla essence and Cointreau.
5. Combine the cream cheese mixture with the cooled custard mixture.
6. Beat the egg whites until they form soft peaks. Slowly add the sugar and continue to beat until stiff. Fold into the cream cheese mixture.
7. Whip the cream until thick and gently fold into the mixture.
8. Pour into the prepared crust and chill until set.

Serves 8.

Chocolate Swirl Cheesecake

Crust:
2 cups crushed graham
   crackers
1½ teaspoons cinnamon
½ cup (125 ml) melted butter

Filling:
1 lb (500 g) cream cheese
1 cup sugar

6 eggs, separated
5 tablespoons plain flour
1½ teaspoons grated lemon
   rind
3 tablespoons lemon juice
1 teaspoon vanilla essence
1 cup (250 ml) cream
2 oz (60 g) dark chocolate

1. Mix together the crushed graham crackers, cinnamon and melted butter. Firmly press on the bottom and sides of 10-inch (25-cm) spring form pan. Chill until ready to use.
2. Soften the cream cheese and beat in the sugar.
3. Add the egg yolks and mix until just blended.
4. Mix in the flour, lemon rind, lemon juice and vanilla essence.
5. Whip the cream and beat the egg whites until stiff. Gently fold the cream and the egg whites into the cream cheese mixture.
6. Grate a little of the chocolate to use as decoration, then melt the rest.
7. Pour one-third of the filling into the prepared crust. Drip half the chocolate over the filling. Pour on the second third of the filling and drip the other half of the chocolate on top. Pour on the remaining filling. Mix through a couple of times with a knife to create the swirls.
8. Bake in a 300°F (150°C) oven for about one hour. Turn off the heat and leave in the oven for another hour. Open the oven door and leave in the oven until completely cool. Decorate with grated chocolate.

Serves 10-12.

Yogurt Cheesecake

Crust:
1½ cups crushed coconut
  cookies
1½ teaspoons cinnamon
2 tablespoons sugar
½ cup (125 ml) melted butter

Filling:
2 tablespoons gelatin
½ cup water
1 lb (500 g) cottage cheese

1 cup (250 g) yogurt
3 eggs, separated
⅔ cup sugar
⅛ teaspoon salt
3 teaspoons grated lemon
  rind
2 tablespoons lemon
  juice
½ cup sugar
1 cup (250 ml) cream

1. Mix together the crushed cookies, cinnamon, sugar and melted butter. Firmly press on the bottom and sides of a 9-inch (23-cm) spring form pan. Chill until ready to use.
2. Mix together the gelatin and water and allow to soak for five minutes.
3. Beat together the cottage cheese and yogurt. Set aside.
4. In the top of a double boiler, beat the egg yolks with the sugar, salt and lemon rind. Put over simmering water and cook, stirring constantly for five minutes.
5. Add the gelatin and stir until dissolved. Remove from heat and cool slightly.
6. Stir in the cheese-yogurt mixture with the lemon juice.
7. Beat the egg whites until they form soft peaks, add the ½ cup sugar and continue beating until stiff. Fold into the cheese-yogurt.
8. Whip the cream and fold into the mixture.
9. Pour into the prepared crust and chill overnight or for eight hours.

Serves 8.

Drambuie Cheesecake

Crust:
1½ cups crushed plain
  vanilla cookies
2½ tablespoons sugar
1 teaspoon cinnamon
½ cup (125 ml) melted butter

Filling:
½ lb (250 g) cottage cheese
½ lb (250 g) cream cheese

1¼ tablespoons gelatin
¼ cup (65 ml) water
1 teaspoon grated lemon rind
4 tablespoons lemon juice
4 tablespoons Drambuie
2 egg whites
½ cup sugar
1½ cups (375 ml) cream
grated chocolate

CONTINUED ON NEXT PAGE

CONTINUED FROM PREVIOUS PAGE

1. Mix together the crushed cookies, sugar, cinnamon and melted butter. Firmly press on the bottom and sides of a 9-inch (23-cm) spring form pan. Chill until ready to use.
2. Press the cottage cheese and cream cheese through a strainer and beat together.
3. Soak the gelatin in the water for five minutes. Place over hot water and stir until dissolved.
4. Add the gelatin to the cheese mixture with the lemon rind, lemon juice and Drambuie. Mix well.
5. Beat the egg whites until they form soft peaks. Slowly add the sugar and continue beating until stiff. Fold into the cheese mixture.
6. Whip the cream and fold into the mixture.
7. Pour into the prepared crust and chill overnight or until firm. Serve decorated with grated chocolate.

Serves 8.

Lemonade Cheesecake

Crust:
1½ cups crushed graham crackers
2½ tablespoons sugar
1½ teaspoons cinnamon
½ cup (125 ml) melted butter

Filling:
¾ cup (185 ml) lemonade
½ cup sugar

1¼ tablespoons gelatin
¾ lb (375 g) cream cheese
1¼ tablespoons grated lemon rind
2½ tablespoons lemon juice
1½ teaspoons vanilla essence
1 cup (250 ml) cream
fresh fruit to decorate

1. Mix together the crushed graham crackers, sugar, cinnamon and melted butter. Firmly press on the bottom of a 9-inch (23-cm) spring form pan. Chill until ready to use.
2. Combine the lemonade, sugar and gelatin in a small saucepan. Place over heat and stir until the sugar and gelatin are dissolved. Set aside until cool.
3. Soften the cream cheese, then beat in the lemon rind, lemon juice and vanilla essence.
4. Mix in the cooled gelatin mixture.
5. Beat the cream and fold into the cheese mixture.
6. Pour into the prepared crust and chill until firm.
7. Serve decorated with fresh fruit of your choice.

Serves 6-8.

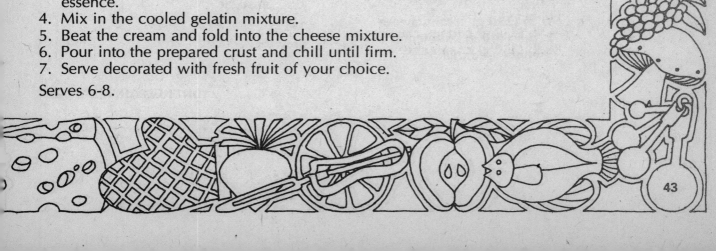

Brandy Cheesecake

Crust:
1½ cups crushed plain
   vanilla cookies
¼ cup ground almonds
4 tablespoons confectioner's sugar
⅓ cup (85 ml) melted butter
1 teaspoon cinnamon
2½ tablespoons brandy

Filling:
2½ tablespoons gelatin

¼ cup (65 ml) water
3 eggs, separated
¾ cup (185 ml) milk
1 cup sugar
1 lb (500 g) cottage cheese
2½ tablespoons lemon juice
2½ tablespoons brandy
1½ cups (375 ml) cream
nutmeg

1. Mix together the crushed cookies, ground almonds, confectioner's sugar, melted butter, cinnamon and brandy. Press on the bottom and sides of a 9-inch (23-cm) spring form pan. Chill until ready to use.
2. Blend the gelatin with the water and allow to soak for five minutes.
3. Combine the egg yolks, milk and sugar in the top of a double boiler. Mix well and put over simmering water. Cook, stirring constantly, until mixture is thick.
4. Add the gelatin and stir until dissolved. Remove from heat.
5. Press the cheese through a strainer and beat with the lemon juice and brandy. Mix into the cottage cheese mixture.
6. Beat the egg whites until stiff and whip the cream.
7. Fold both the egg whites and the cream into the cottage cheese mixture.
8. Pour into the prepared crust and chill until set.

Serves 8.

Meringue Topped Cheesecake

Crust:
1½ cups crushed plain
   vanilla cookies
2½ tablespoons sugar
1½ teaspoons cinnamon
½ cup (125 ml) melted butter

Filling:
½ lb (250 g) cream cheese
1 can (440 g) sweetened
   condensed milk

3 egg yolks
1¼ tablespoons grated lemon
   rind
4 tablespoons lemon juice

Meringue Topping:
3 egg whites
⅔ cup sugar

CONTINUED ON NEXT PAGE

CONTINUED FROM PREVIOUS PAGE

1. Mix together the crushed cookies, sugar, cinnamon and melted butter. Firmly press on the bottom and sides of a 9-inch (23-cm) spring form pan. Chill until ready to use.
2. Soften the cream cheese and beat in the condensed milk, lightly beaten egg yolks, lemon rind and lemon juice.
3. Pour into the prepared crust.
4. Beat the egg whites until they form soft peaks. Slowly add half the sugar and beat until stiff. Fold in the remaining sugar and spread over the cheese filling.
5. Bake in a 400°F (200°C) oven for about ten minutes or until the meringue is golden brown. Cool.

Serves 8.

Rich Chocolate Cheesecake

Crust:
1½ cups crushed chocolate
   cookies
¼ teaspoon nutmeg
½ cup (125 ml) melted butter

Filling:
6 oz (185 g) dark chocolate
1 lb (500 g) cream cheese

¾ cup sugar
3 eggs
1¼ tablespoons cocoa
1½ teaspoons vanilla essence
1 cup (250 g) sour cream
½ cup (125 ml) cream
grated chocolate

1. Mix together the crushed cookies, nutmeg and melted butter. Firmly press on the bottom of a 9-inch (23-cm) spring form pan.
2. Melt the chocolate in a small bowl over hot water.
3. Press the cream cheese through a strainer and beat in the sugar until the mixture is smooth.
4. Add the eggs one at a time, beating well after each addition.
5. Mix in the melted chocolate, cocoa, vanilla essence and sour cream.
6. Beat the cream and fold into the chocolate mixture.
7. Pour into the prepared crust and bake in a 300°F (150°C) oven for about one hour. Turn off the heat and leave the cake in the oven with the door closed for 30 minutes. Open the door and leave the cake until it is cool.
8. Serve sprinkled with grated chocolate.

Serves 8.

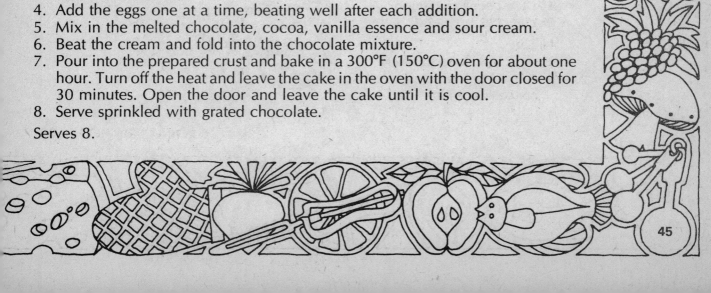

Blackberry-Glazed Cheesecake

Crust:
1½ cups crushed graham crackers
4 tablespoons sugar
1½ teaspoons cinnamon
½ cup (125 ml) melted butter

Filling:
1½ lb (750 g) cream cheese
4 tablespoons cake flour
1 tablespoon grated lemon rind

1¼ tablespoons lemon juice
⅔ cup (165 ml) sour cream
2 eggs
¾ cup sugar
¾ cup (185 ml) milk

Glaze:
250 g (½ lb) blackberries
½ cup (125 ml) water
3 tablespoons cornstarch
⅓ cup sugar

1. Mix together the crushed graham crackers, sugar, cinnamon and melted butter. Press firmly on the bottom of a 9-inch (23-cm) spring form pan. Chill until ready to use.
2. Press the cream cheese through a strainer, then beat in the flour, lemon rind, lemon juice and sour cream.
3. Beat the eggs with the sugar until light and fluffy.
4. Add the milk to the egg mixture and beat thoroughly.
5. Slowly add the cheese mixture to the egg mixture beating well.
6. Pour into the prepared crust and bake in a 325°F (160°C) oven for about 1½ hours. Turn off the heat and leave the cheesecake in the oven with the door open until cool.
7. Crush the blackberries and mix with the water in a saucepan. Cook for five minutes. Strain.
8. Mix the cornstarch with the sugar and stir into the strained liquid. Cook over a medium heat, stirring constantly, until the mixture thickens. Cool slightly then pour over the cheesecake. Chill. (If the glaze is not thick enough, add a little more cornstarch mixed with water.)

Serves 10.

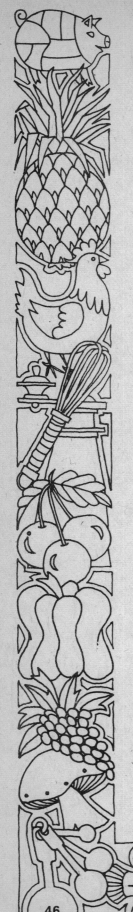

Pies and Flans

Blender Cheese Pie

Crust:
2 cups finely crushed
  graham crackers
½ cup (125 ml) melted butter
2½ tablespoons sugar

Filling:
¾ lb (375 g) cream cheese
2 eggs
2½ tablespoons milk

¼ cup sugar
1 ¼ tablespoons lemon juice
1 teaspoon vanilla essence
1 teaspoon grated lemon rind

Topping:
1 cup (250 g) sour cream
¼ cup sugar
1 teaspoon vanilla

1. Mix together the crushed graham crackers, butter and sugar. If the mixture is too dry, add a little more melted butter.
2. Firmly press on the bottom and sides of a 9-inch (23-cm) pie tin. Set aside.
3. Put the remaining ingredients into an electric blender and whirl for one minute or longer if all the ingredients are not completely blended.
4. Pour into the pie shell and bake in a 375°F (190°C) oven for about 23 minutes. Cool.
5. Make the topping by combining all the topping ingredients. Spread over the baked and cooled pie. Put in a 475°F (250°C) oven for seven minutes. Cool and serve.

Serves 8.

Jello Cheese Pie

Pastry:
1 cup plain flour
½ teaspoon salt
⅓ cup (85 g) butter
3 tablespoons cold water

Filling:
1¼ tablespoons gelatin
¼ cup (65 ml) water
2 eggs, separated
1 cup sugar
⅓ cup (85 ml) milk
1½ teaspoons grated lemon
   rind

1½ teaspoons grated orange
   rind
¼ cup (65 ml) lemon juice
¼ cup (65 ml) orange juice
½ lb (250 g) cream cheese
1 cup (250 ml) cream
1 cup chopped orange
   segments
1 cup (250 ml) orange juice
1 cup (250 ml) water
1 pack lemon jello

1. Sift the flour with the salt and rub in the butter until the mixture is the consistency of fine bread crumbs. Add the water and mix only until the pastry holds together.
2. Roll out and line a 9-inch (23-cm) pie tin. Bake in a 400°F (200°C) oven until golden brown.
3. Mix the gelatin with the water and allow to soak for five minutes.
4. Beat the egg yolks with half the sugar in the top of a double boiler.
5. Add the milk and mix well. Cook, stirring constantly, over simmering water until the sugar dissolves and the mixture is slightly thickened.
6. Add the gelatin and stir until the gelatin is dissolved.
7. Add the grated rinds and the orange and lemon juices.
8. In a large bowl soften the cream cheese. Gradually add the gelatin mixture.
9. Beat the egg whites until stiff. Gradually add the sugar and continue beating until the sugar is dissolved. Gently fold into the cream cheese mixture.
10. Lightly beat the cream and fold into the mixture. Pour into the pastry shell and chill.
11. Spread the orange pieces on top of the pie.
12. Heat the orange juice and water and add the lemon jello. Stir until dissolved. Cool, then chill until thick. Spoon over the pie and chill until set.

Serves 8.

Easy Lemon Cheese Pie

Crust:
1½ cups corn flake crumbs
6 tablespoons sugar
1 teaspoon cinnamon
⅓ cup (85 ml) melted butter

Filling:
½ lb (250 g) cream cheese

1 cup (250 ml) milk
1 cup (250 ml) cream
1 pack lemon instant
  pudding
1½ teaspoons vanilla essence
1½ teaspoons grated lemon
  rind

1. Mix the corn flake crumbs with the sugar, cinnamon and melted butter. Press on the bottom and sides of a 8-inch (20-cm) pie tin. Bake in a 350°F (180°C) oven for ten minutes. Cool.
2. Thoroughly beat together all the filling ingredients.
3. Pour into the prepared crust and chill for at least one hour.

Serves 6-8.

Orange-Cheese Pie

Pastry:
1 cup plain flour
½ teaspoon salt
⅓ cup (85 g) butter
3 tablespoons cold water

Filling:
½ lb (250 g) cream cheese

2 eggs, beaten
½ cup sugar
4 tablespoons orange juice
1½ teaspoons grated orange
  rind
1 teaspoon grated lemon rind
whipped cream

1. Sift together the flour and salt. Mix in the butter until the mixture is the consistency of bread crumbs. Add the water and mix to a firm dough. Roll out and line a 9-inch (23-cm) pie tin. Bake in a 400°F (200°C) oven until golden brown.
2. Soften the cream cheese and add the eggs. Beat until smooth.
3. Add the sugar, orange juice, grated orange and lemon rinds. Mix well.
4. Pour into the baked pie shell and bake in a 350°F (180°C) oven for about 20 minutes or until firm. Cool before serving.
5. Garnish with whipped cream.

Serves 6-8.

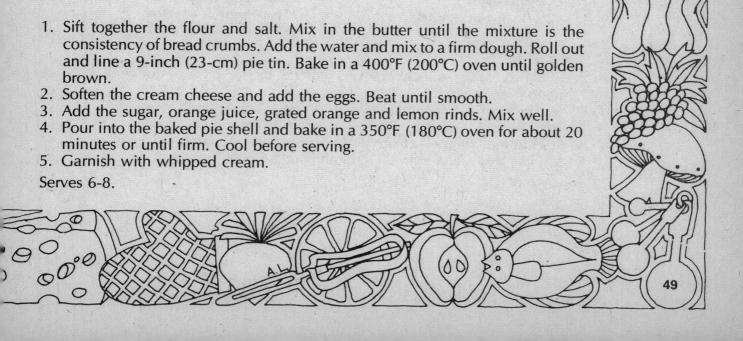

Raspberry Flan

Crust:
2 cups crushed graham
crackers
4 tablespoons sugar
½ cup (125 ml) melted butter
1½ teaspoons cinnamon

Filling:
½ lb (250 g) cream cheese

¼ cup sugar
¾ cup (185 ml) cream
1 tablespoon gelatin
½ cup (125 ml) water
1 can (425 g) raspberries or
fresh in season
whipped cream to decorate

1. Mix together the graham cracker crumbs, sugar, melted butter and cinnamon. Press into a flan dish.
2. Beat the cream cheese with the sugar until smooth.
3. Whip the cream and gently fold into the cheese mixture.
4. Soak the gelatin in the water for five minutes. Put over hot water and stir until dissolved. Mix into the cream cheese mixture.
5. Drain the raspberries and fold into the mixture.
6. Pour into the prepared crust and chill for a couple of hours.
7. Before serving decorate with whipped cream. Serves 6-8.

Fruit Salad Cheese Pie

1 cup crushed graham
crackers
4 tablespoons (60 ml) melted
butter

Filling:
½ lb (250 g) cream cheese
¾ cup sugar
2½ teaspoons grated lemon
rind

1 teaspoon grated orange
rind
2 teaspoons lemon juice
½ cup desiccated coconut
1 cup (250 ml) cream,
whipped

Topping:
2 cups fresh fruit salad
⅓ cup strawberry jam

1. Mix the crushed graham crackers with the melted butter. Firmly press on the bottom of a 9-inch (23-cm) pie tin.
2. Soften the cream cheese and beat with the sugar until smooth.
3. Add the lemon and orange rinds, lemon juice and coconut.
4. Fold in the whipped cream and pour into the prepared crust.
5. Mix the fruit salad with the jam and spread over the top of the cheese pie.

Serves 6-8.

Cherry Cheese Pie

Pastry:
1¼ cups plain flour
¼ cup sugar
½ cup (125 g) butter
1 egg yolk, beaten
½ teaspoon vanilla essence

Filling:
½ lb (250 g) cream cheese

½ lb (250 g) cottage cheese
¾ cup sugar
1½ teaspoons vanilla essence
⅛ teaspoon nutmeg
2 eggs
½ teaspoon cinnamon
1 can (645 g) cherry pie filling

1. Sift together the flour and sugar. Add the butter and mix until the consistency of fine bread crumbs.
2. Add the egg yolk and vanilla and mix until the pastry just holds together.
3. Roll out and line a 9-inch (23-cm) pie tin. Set aside.
4. Mix the cream cheese until soft and smooth.
5. Add the cottage cheese, sugar, vanilla and nutmeg and beat well.
6. Add the eggs one at a time, beating well after each addition.
7. Pour the cheese mixture into the prepared pie shell and bake in a 350°F (180°C) oven for 45 minutes.
8. Mix the cinnamon with the cherry pie filling and spread over the top of the pie. Cool.

Serves 8.

Quick Cheese Pie

½ lb (250 g) cream cheese
½ cup sugar
1½ teaspoons vanilla essence
1 cup (250 ml) cream
1 pastry shell
1 cup sliced bananas (or fruit of your choice)

1. Beat together the cream cheese, sugar and vanilla.
2. Whip the cream and fold into the cream cheese mixture.
3. Pour into the pastry shell and chill.
4. Top with fruit and serve immediately.

Serves 6.

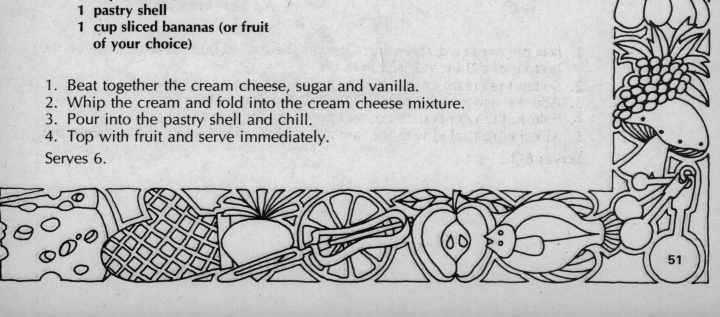

Chestnut Cheese Pie

Pastry:
1 cup plain flour
¼ cup sugar
1 teaspoon grated lemon rind
1 egg yolk
½ cup (125 g) butter

Filling:
½ lb (250 g) chestnut puree
½ lb (250 g) cream cheese
½ cup (125 ml) sweetened
   condensed milk

2½ tablespoons lemon juice
1 teaspoon vinegar
⅔ cup (165 ml) cream
2 teaspoons brandy

Topping:
¼ cup (65 ml) water
½ cup sugar
2 tablespoons cream
1 teaspoon brandy
½ lb (250 g) chestnut puree

1. Sift together the flour and sugar. Add the lemon rind, egg yolk and butter and mix well. Roll out and line a 9-inch (23-cm) pie tin. Prick the bottom with a fork and bake in a 400°F (200°C) oven until golden brown. Cool.
2. Sieve the chestnut puree and the cream cheese, then beat together until smooth.
3. Add the condensed milk, lemon juice and vinegar. Mix well.
4. Whip the cream and fold into the mixture with the brandy.
5. Pour into the prepared cooled pastry shell and chill until firm.
6. Mix together the water and sugar in a saucepan and bring to a boil, stirring constantly until the sugar has dissolved. Boil without stirring until the mixture is at the soft ball stage. (Soft ball stage is when a drop of the sugar mixture forms a soft ball when dropped into a glass of cold water.) Remove from heat.
7. Mix together the cream, brandy and sieved chestnut puree.
8. Add the sugar syrup and mix well.
9. Spread over the chilled pie and refrigerate until the topping is set.

Serves 8.

Glazed Cheese Pie

Pastry:
¾ cup cake flour
pinch of salt
¼ cup (65 g) butter
ice water

Filling:
½ lb (250 g) cream cheese

½ cup sugar
2½ tablespoons plain flour
2 eggs
⅓ cup (85 ml) milk
1 teaspoon vanilla essence

1. Sift together the flour and salt. Cut in the butter and mix until the mixture is the consistency of bread crumbs. Add just enough ice water to make a firm dough. Roll out on a floured board and line a 9-inch (23-cm) pie tin. Set aside.
2. Cream the cheese until soft.
3. Gradually add the sugar.
4. Stir in the flour and the eggs. Mix thoroughly.
5. Add the milk and vanilla and beat well.
6. Pour into the unbaked pie shell and bake in a 350°F (180°C) oven for about 40 minutes.
7. Cool and glaze with one of the glazes below.

Serves 6.

Pineapple Glaze: Cook together 1 cup (250 ml) pineapple juice, 1¼ tablespoons cornstarch and one tablespoon sugar. Mix in ½ cup drained crushed pineapple and one teaspoon vanilla essence. Pour over the cooled pie and put into the refrigerator.

Peach Glaze: Cook together until bubbly ¾ cup (185 ml) peach syrup (from the can of peaches) and 2½ tablespoons cornstarch. Add one teaspoon almond extract. Arrange peach slices on top of the cooled pie and pour cooked glaze over the top. Put into the refrigerator.

Cherry Glaze: Cook together one cup (250 ml) cherry juice from the canned cherries and 1¼ tablespoons cornstarch. Add one tablespoon sugar. Mix in one teaspoon almond extract and one cup of cherries. Pour over the cooled pie and put into the refrigerator.

Currant Cottage Cheese Pie

Pastry:
1 cup plain flour
¼ cup sugar
grated rind of one lemon
1 egg yolk
½ cup (125 g) butter

Filling:
¾ lb (375 g) cottage cheese
1¼ tablespoons plain flour

⅛ teaspoon salt
1 cup (250 ml) cream
⅔ cup sugar
grated rind of one lemon
4 tablespoons lemon juice
3 eggs, separated
½ cup dried currants
confectioner's sugar

1. Mix together the flour and sugar. Add the lemon rind, egg yolk and butter. Mix well and roll out. Line a 9-inch (23-cm) pie tin with the pastry.
2. Force the cheese through a fine strainer.
3. Blend in the flour and salt. Mix well.
4. Add the cream, sugar, lemon rind and lemon juice.
5. Beat the egg yolks until thick and light yellow colored. Mix with the currants and stir into the cheese mixture.
6. Beat the egg whites until stiff and fold into the mixture. Pour into the pie shell.
7. Bake in a 450°F (230°C) oven for ten minutes. Reduce the heat to 350°F (180°C) and cook for another 45 minutes. Cool and sprinkle with confectioner's sugar.

Serves 6-8.

Coffee Cheese Pie

Pastry:
1 cup plain flour
¼ cup sugar
⅓ cup (85 g) butter
1 egg yolk
½ teaspoon vanilla essence

Filling:
½ lb (250 g) cottage cheese
½ lb (250 g) cream cheese
1¼ tablespoons gelatin

¼ cup (65 ml) cold water
¼ cup (65 ml) boiling water
1 tablespoon instant coffee powder
3 teaspoons grated lemon rind
2 tablespoons lemon juice
1½ cups (375 ml) cream
2 egg whites
½ cup sugar

CONTINUED ON NEXT PAGE

CONTINUED FROM PREVIOUS PAGE

1. Sift together the flour and sugar. Rub in the butter until the mixture resembles fine bread crumbs. Add the egg yolk and vanilla essence and mix to a firm dough. (If the mixture is too dry, add a little water.) Roll out and line a 9-inch (23-cm) pie tin. Bake the pastry in a 400°F (200°C) oven for 10-15 minutes or until golden brown. Cool.
2. Press the cottage cheese and cream cheese through a strainer. Beat together until smooth.
3. Soak the gelatin in the cold water for five minutes. Add the boiling water and stir until dissolved.
4. Mix the cheese with the instant coffee powder, lemon rind, lemon juice and gelatin.
5. Whip the cream and fold into the cheese mixture.
6. Beat the egg whites until they form soft peaks. Slowly add the sugar continuing to beat until stiff. Fold into the cheese mixture.
7. Pour into the cooled pastry and chill until firm.

Serves 8.

Almond Cheese Pie

Crust:
1½ cups crushed plain
   vanilla cookies
2 teaspoons cinnamon
2½ tablespoons sugar
½ cup (125 ml) melted butter

Filling:
½ lb (250 g) cream cheese
⅓ cup sugar

2 eggs, separated
½ cup (55 g) ground almonds
2½ tablespoons semolina
⅓ cup raisins, chopped
2 teaspoons grated lemon
   rind
4 tablespoons lemon juice
¼ cup (65 ml) cream
blanched almonds

1. Mix together the crushed cookies, cinnamon, sugar and melted butter. Firmly press on the bottom and sides of a 9-inch (23-cm) pie tin.
2. Soften the cream cheese and beat in the sugar.
3. Lightly beat the egg yolks and add to the cream cheese mixture with the ground almonds, semolina, raisins, lemon rind and lemon juice.
4. Whip the cream and add to the mixture.
5. Beat the egg whites until stiff and gently fold into the pie mixture.
6. Pour into the prepared crust and bake in a 300°F (150°C) oven for about one hour. Turn off the heat, decorate with the almonds and allow to cool in the oven with the door open.

Serves 6-8.

Apple Cheese Pie

Pastry:
- 1½ cups plain flour
- ¼ teaspoon salt
- ½ teaspoon cinnamon
- 4 tablespoons sugar
- 1¼ teaspoons baking powder
- 1½ teaspoons grated lemon rind
- ½ cup (125 g) butter
- 1 egg yolk
- 2½ tablespoons sherry

Filling:
- 2 cooking apples
- 2 eggs
- ⅔ cup sugar
- 2½ tablespoons plain flour
- 2½ teaspoons grated lemon rind
- ⅔ cup (165 ml) cream
- 4 tablespoons raisins
- ⅛ teaspoon salt
- ½ lb (250 g) cream cheese

1. Sift together the flour, salt, cinnamon, sugar and baking powder. Stir in the grated lemon rind. Add the butter and mix until it is the consistency of bread crumbs. Beat the egg yolk with the sherry and mix into the flour mixture. Roll out and line a 9-inch (23-cm) pie tin. Trim the edges.
2. Peel and core the apples and cut into thin slices. Arrange on the base of the pastry shell.
3. Beat together the eggs and sugar until thick.
4. Add the flour, lemon rind, cream, raisins, salt and cream cheese. Mix until smooth.
5. Pour over the apples and bake in a 350°F (180°C) oven for about one hour. Turn off the heat and allow to cool in the oven with the door open.

Serves 6-8.

Raisin Cheese Pie

Pastry:
- 1 cup plain flour
- ½ cup cake flour
- 2 tablespoons custard powder
- 3 tablespoons cornstarch
- 2 tablespoons confectioner's sugar
- ½ cup (125 g) butter
- cold water

Filling:
- ½ lb (250 g) cottage cheese
- 3 tablespoons (45 g) butter
- 4 tablespoon sugar
- 1 egg
- 2 tablespoons milk
- 3 teaspoons grated lemon rind
- ½ cup raisins

CONTINUED ON NEXT PAGE

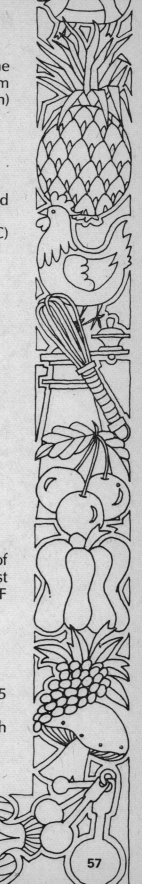

CONTINUED FROM PREVIOUS PAGE

1. Sift together dry ingredients and rub in the butter until the mixture is the consistency of fine bread crumbs. Add just enough cold water to form a firm dough. Chill for one hour. Roll out ⅔ of the pastry and line a 8-inch (20-cm) pie tin.
2. Press the cottage cheese through a strainer.
3. Cream together butter and sugar until light and fluffy.
4. Add the egg and beat well.
5. Mix in the cheese, milk, lemon rind and raisins. Pour into the prepared pastry.
6. Roll out the remaining pastry and place on top of the pie. Trim the edges and prick in several places to allow steam to escape.
7. Bake in a 400°F (200°C) oven for 15 minutes. Reduce heat to 350°F (180°C) and bake for another ½ hour. Cool and chill.

Serves 6-8.

Choc-Rum Cheese Pie

Pastry:
1¼ cups plain flour
¼ cup sugar
½ cup (125 g) butter
1 egg yolk, beaten
½ teaspoon vanilla essence

Filling:
1 lb (500 g) cream cheese
3 eggs

½ cup sugar
½ teaspoon vanilla
2 oz (60 g) dark chocolate, melted
2 tablespoons rum

Topping:
1 cup (250 ml) cream
1½ tablespoons rum
nutmeg

1. Sift together the flour and sugar. Add the butter and mix until the consistency of fine bread crumbs. Add the egg yolk and vanilla and mix until the pastry just holds together. Roll out and line a 9-inch (23-cm) pie tin. Bake in a 400°F (200°C) oven for ten minutes.
2. Press the cream cheese through a fine strainer.
3. Mix together the eggs and sugar until thick and light yellow colored.
4. Add the cream cheese and mix until smooth.
5. Mix in the vanilla, melted chocolate and rum.
6. Pour into the pastry shell and bake in a 350°F (180°C) oven for about 45 minutes. Cool.
7. Whip the cream and add the rum. Spread over the cooled pie and sprinkle with nutmeg.

Serves 6-8.

Passionfruit Cheese Pie

Pastry:
1½ cups plain flour
⅛ teaspoon salt
½ teaspoon baking powder
½ cup (125 g) butter
water

Filling:
1 lb (500 g) cream cheese
½ cup sugar

3 eggs, separated
4 tablespoons plain flour
2 teaspoons grated lemon rind
2 tablespoons lemon juice
1 teaspoon vanilla essence
½ cup (125 ml) cream
pulp of 4 passion fruit

1. Sift the flour and the salt and rub the butter in until the mixture resembles fine bread crumbs. Add just enough water to form a firm dough. Roll out and line a 9-inch (23-cm) pie tin. Bake in a 400°F (200°C) oven for ten minutes.
2. Soften the cream cheese and beat in the sugar until the mixture is smooth.
3. Lightly beat the egg yolks and mix into the cheese until just blended.
4. Stir in the flour, lemon rind, lemon juice and vanilla.
5. Whip the cream and fold into the mixture.
6. Beat the egg whites until stiff and fold into the mixture with the pulp of three passionfruit.
7. Pour into the prepared pastry shell and bake in a 300°F (150°C) oven for one hour. Turn off the heat and leave the pie in the oven until cool.
8. Serve topped with the remaining passionfruit pulp.

Serves 8.

Cheese Torte

Crust:
2 cups crushed vanilla cookies
½ cup sugar
1 teaspoon cinnamon
½ cup (125 ml) melted butter

Filling:
4 eggs
1 cup sugar

⅛ teaspoon salt
3 tablespoons lemon juice
grated rind of one lemon
1 teaspoon vanilla essence
1 cup (250 ml) cream
750 g (1½ lb) cottage cheese
¾ cup plain flour
½ cup whole toasted almonds

1. Make the pie shell by mixing the crushed cookies with the sugar, cinnamon and melted butter. Set aside a little to sprinkle on the top of the torte. Butter a 9-inch (23-cm) spring form pan. Press the mixture on the bottom and sides of the pan. Set aside.
2. Beat the eggs with the sugar until light.
3. Add the salt, lemon juice, lemon rind and vanilla and mix thoroughly.
4. Add the cream, cheese and flour and mix well. Strain through a fine sieve or whirl in an electric blender.
5. Pour into the pie shell and sprinkle with the reserved crumb mixture.
6. Bake in a 325°F (160°C) oven for one hour. Turn off the heat and leave in the oven for another hour. Open the oven door for the last ½ hour. If the torte is not cooled this slowly, it will fall.
7. Garnish with almonds and remove the rim of the spring form pan.

Serves 10.

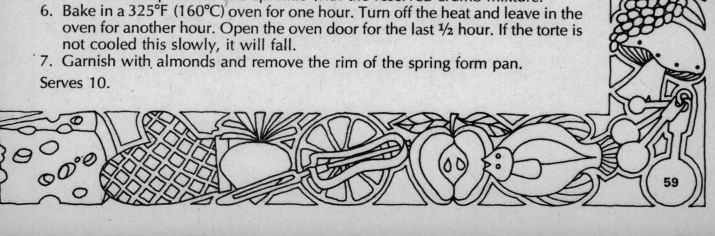

Orange Cheese Torte

1 sponge cake
1 lb (500 g) cream cheese
½ cup sugar
¼ cup citron
1½ tablespoons grated orange
    rind

¼ cup (65 ml) orange juice
2 teaspoons rum
3 tablespoons melted
    chocolate

1. Cut the sponge cake into three layers.
2. Thoroughly mix together the cream cheese and sugar.
3. Stir in the citron and orange rind. Set aside.
4. In a separate bowl mix together the orange juice and rum.
5. Sprinkle ⅓ of the orange and rum mixture on the bottom layer of cake.
6. Spread half the cheese mixture on top. Put the second layer of cake on and repeat the process.
7. Top with the third layer and sprinkle on the remaining ⅓ of the orange and rum mixture.
8. Dribble the chocolate on the top allowing it to drip down the sides.

Serves 8-10.

Slices and Bars

Apricot Cheese Fingers

Pastry:
2 cups plain flour
½ cup (125 g) butter
3 tablespoons sugar
1 egg
milk

Filling:
1 cup chopped dried apricots
2 tablespoons sugar

¾ lb (375 g) cream cheese
4 tablespoons (60 g) butter
4 tablespoons sugar
3 eggs, separated
1¼ tablespoons milk
1¼ tablespoons grated lemon rind
1½ tablespoons lemon juice

1. Sift the flour and cut in the butter. Add the sugar, slightly beaten egg and enough milk to form a firm dough. Chill for one hour. Divide into two equal portions. Roll out one half and line a buttered 7×10-inch (18×25-cm) tin. Bake in a 350°F (180°C) oven for ten minutes.
2. Soak the apricots in enough water to cover for ½ hour.
3. Add the 2 tablespoons sugar and simmer until tender. Drain and cool. Spread over cooked pastry.
4. Press the cream cheese through a strainer.
5. Beat together the butter and sugar until light.
6. Beat in the egg yolks, milk, lemon rind, lemon juice and cream cheese.
7. Beat the egg whites until they form soft peaks and fold into the cheese mixture. Spread over the apricots.
8. Roll out the other half of the dough and place on top of the filling. Prick in several places to allow steam to escape.
9. Bake in a 350°F (180°C) oven for about ½ hour. Cool and cut into fingers.

Raspberry Cheese Squares

Crust:
1½ cups crushed graham
   crackers
1 teaspoon cinnamon
½ cup (125 ml) melted butter

Filling:
raspberry jam
½ cup brown sugar
1½ tablespoons cornstarch

½ teaspoon cinnamon
¾ lb (375 g) cream cheese
¼ teaspoon salt
3 teaspoons grated lemon
   rind
2 tablespoons lemon juice
3 eggs, separated
1 cup (250 g) sour cream
½ cup sugar

1. Mix together the crushed graham crackers, cinnamon and melted butter. Firmly press on the bottom of a buttered 7 × 10-inch (18 × 25-cm) tin.
2. Spread a thick layer of raspberry jam on the crumb crust.
3. Mix the brown sugar with the cornstarch and cinnamon.
4. Soften the cream cheese and mix with the brown sugar mixture.
5. Add the salt, lemon rind and lemon juice and mix well.
6. Lightly beat the egg yolks and stir into the cream cheese mixture with the sour cream.
7. Beat the egg whites until frothy, then add the sugar slowly and continue beating until stiff. Fold into the cream cheese mixture. Pour over the prepared crust and smooth out.
8. Bake in a 350°F (180°C) oven for ½ hour. Reduce the heat to 300°F (150°C) and cook for another 35 minutes. Turn off the heat and leave in the oven until cool. Cut into squares and serve.

Grapefruit Cheese Slice

Crust:
1½ cups crushed vanilla
 cookies
1 teaspoon cinnamon
1½ tablespoons sugar
½ cup (125 ml) melted butter

Filling:
1¼ tablespoons gelatin
¼ cup (65 ml) water
⅓ cup (85 ml) boiling water
¾ lb (375 g) cream cheese
⅓ cup sugar
½ cup (125 ml) grapefruit
 juice

1 tablespoon grated
 grapefruit rind
1 tablespoon grated orange
 rind
2 egg whites

Glaze:
1 tablespoon gelatin
¼ cup (65 ml) water
½ cup sugar
1 cup (250 ml) grapefruit
 juice

1. Mix together the crushed cookies, cinnamon, sugar and melted butter. Press firmly on the bottom of a 7 × 10-inch (18 × 25-cm) tin lined with aluminum foil. Chill until ready to use.
2. Soak the gelatin in the water for five minutes. Add the boiling water and stir until dissolved. Cool.
3. Soften the cream cheese, then beat in the sugar until smooth.
4. Add the grapefruit juice and rinds and mix well.
5. Beat the egg whites until they form soft peaks, then fold into the cream cheese mixture. Spread on the prepared crust.
6. Mix the gelatin with the water and allow to soak for five minutes.
7. Mix the sugar and grapefruit juice in a saucepan and heat until the sugar dissolves.
8. Add the gelatin and cook until the glaze is clear. Cool and pour on top of the filling. Refrigerate until firm. Cut into slices and serve.

Peach-Cheese Roll

4 eggs, beaten
¾ cup sugar
½ teaspoon vanilla essence
1 cup plain flour
1¼ teaspoons baking powder
¼ teaspoon salt
½ teaspoon cinnamon

¼ teaspoon nutmeg
¼ lb (125 g) cream cheese
½ lb (250 g) cottage cheese
½ cup confectioner's sugar
2 tablespoons lemon juice
4 peaches, peeled and thinly sliced

1. Beat together the eggs and sugar until light and fluffy. Add the vanilla.
2. Sift together the flour, baking powder, salt, cinnamon and nutmeg. Fold into the egg mixture.
3. Pour into a Swiss-roll tin lined with buttered wax paper.
4. Bake in a 400°F (200°C) oven for about 15 minutes.
5. Turn out the cake onto a tea towel sprinkled with confectioner's sugar. Remove wax paper and trim the edges. Roll the cake up and wrap in the tea towel. Cool.
6. Beat together the cream cheese and cottage cheese.
7. Add the confectioner's sugar and lemon juice and beat until fluffy.
8. Unroll the cake and evenly spread on the cheese mixture. Arrange the peach slices on top and roll the cake up again. Chill. Serve in slices. Serves 8.

Lemon Cheese Fingers

Crust:
1½ cups crushed vanilla cookies
2 teaspoons grated lemon rind
½ cup (125 ml) melted butter

Filling:
½ lb (250 g) cream cheese

2 eggs, separated
2 teaspoons grated lemon rind
2½ tablespoons lemon juice
⅓ cup sugar
2 tablespoons citron

1. Mix together the crushed cookies, lemon rind and melted butter. Press onto the bottom of a 7 × 10-inch (18 × 25-cm) tin. Chill until ready to use.
2. Soften the cream cheese and beat in the egg yolks until smooth.
3. Add the lemon rind, lemon juice, sugar and citron. Blend thoroughly.
4. Beat the egg whites lightly and fold into the cream cheese mixture. Spread over the prepared crust.
5. Bake in a 350°F (180°C) oven for about ½ hour. Cool and cut into fingers.

Sultana Raisin Cream Cheese Squares

Pastry:
2 cups plain flour
½ teaspoon baking powder
½ cup (125 g) butter
⅛ teaspoon salt
1 egg yolk
2 tablespoons lemon juice
1 teaspoon vanilla essence
water

Filling:
2½ cups (625 ml) milk
4 eggs
½ lb (250 g) cream cheese
½ cup sugar
1½ teaspoons vanilla essence
½ cup (125 ml) cream
2 tablespoons lemon juice
¾ cup sultana raisins

1. Sift together the flour and baking powder. Rub in the butter until the mixture resembles fine bread crumbs. Mix together the salt, egg yolk, lemon juice and vanilla essence. Add to the flour mixture and mix to a firm dough. If necessary, add a little water. Roll out and line a 7 × 10-inch (18 × 25-cm) tin. Prick the pastry and bake in a 350°F (180°C) oven for ten minutes. Cool.
2. Warm the milk slightly.
3. Beat the eggs lightly and slowly add half the milk, stirring constantly.
4. Soften the cream cheese, then beat in the sugar and vanilla essence until smooth.
5. Add the remaining milk to the cream cheese mixture. Mix well, then add the egg mixture and blend thoroughly.
6. Beat in cream, lemon juice and sultana raisins. Pour into prepared pastry.
7. Bake in a 400°F (200°C) oven for ten minutes. Reduce the heat to 300°F (150°C) and bake for another 40 minutes. Cool and cut into squares.

Pascha

2 egg yolks
½ cup sugar
1 lb (500 g) dry cottage cheese
⅓ cup (85 g) butter
⅓ cup (85 ml) cream

grated rind of one lemon
¼ teaspoon vanilla essence
½ teaspoon almond extract
madeira cake

1. In a saucepan beat together the egg yolks and sugar.
2. Add the cheese, butter, cream and lemon rind and mix well. Bring to a boil. Reduce heat and simmer for five minutes, stirring constantly.
3. Remove from the heat and cool slightly. Stir in the vanilla and almond extract.
4. Line a strainer or colander with three thicknesses of cheesecloth. Put over a bowl. Pour in the cheese mixture and tie up. Cover and put into the refrigerator. Allow to drain until moisture drips out. Untie the cloth and put on a plate. Remove cloth.
5. Serve spread on slices of madeira cake. (Especially good served on toasted cake.)

Serves 6.

Cheese-Jam Turnovers

½ lb (250 g) cream cheese
½ cup (125 g) butter
1½ cups plain flour
½ teaspoon salt
raspberry or strawberry jam
½ lb (250 g) cream cheese
1 egg, beaten

1. Blend together the cream cheese and the butter.
2. Add the flour and salt and mix well. Chill for several hours or overnight.
3. Roll out the dough to a 16-inch (40-cm) square then cut into 25 squares.
4. Put a small amount of jam and a piece of cream cheese on one side of each square. Moisten edges and fold over to form oblongs or triangles. Press edges together with a fork and brush with the beaten egg.
5. Bake in a 450°F (230°C) oven for about 15 minutes.

Chocolate Royale

Crust:
1 cup chocolate cookie
   crumbs
¼ cup finely chopped walnuts
¼ cup (65 ml) melted butter

Filling:
1 tablespoon gelatin
½ cup (125 ml) water
½ lb (250 g) cream cheese
1 cup sugar

2 teaspoons vanilla essence
½ teaspoon peppermint
   essence
½ lb (250 g) cooking
   chocolate
1 cup (250 ml) cream,
   whipped
chopped nuts
glace cherries, chopped

1. Mix together the cookie crumbs, walnuts and melted butter. Firmly press on the bottom of a 9-inch (23-cm) spring form pan. Bake in a 350°F (180°C) oven for about ten minutes. Cool.
2. Mix the gelatin with the water and allow to soak for five minutes. Place over hot water and stir until dissolved.
3. Soften the cream cheese and beat in sugar, vanilla and peppermint essences.
4. Melt the chocolate and add to the cream cheese mixture with the dissolved gelatin. Beat well.
5. Fold in the whipped cream and pour into the prepared crust. Chill until firm.
6. Serve sprinkled with chopped nuts and glace cherries.

Serves 8.

Gooseberry Slice

Crust:
1½ cups crushed graham
    crackers
4 tablespoons sugar
1 teaspoon cinnamon
½ cup (125 ml) melted butter

Filling:
1 pack lemon jello
1¾ cups (435 ml) boiling
    water

2 teaspoons grated lemon
    rind
½ lb (250 g) cream cheese
½ teaspoon vanilla essence
1½ cups (375 ml) cream
4 Chinese gooseberries,
    peeled and chopped

1. Mix together the crushed graham crackers, sugar, cinnamon and melted butter. Press firmly on the bottom of a 7 × 10-inch (18 × 25-cm) tin. Chill until ready to use.
2. Mix the jello with the boiling water. Stir until dissolved. Cool.
3. Combine 1 teaspoon grated lemon rind with the cream cheese and vanilla essence. Mix until smooth.
4. Mix 1¼ cups of the jello mixture with the cream cheese mixture.
5. Beat the cream and fold into the cheese mixture. Pour onto the prepared crust. Chill until firm.
6. Mix the remaining jello with the gooseberries and spread on top. Refrigerate until set. Cut into slices and serve.

Passionfruit Slice

Crust:
1½ cups crushed plain
   vanilla cookies
½ cup desiccated coconut
⅔ cup (165 ml) melted butter

Filling:
1¼ tablespoons gelatin
¼ cup (65 ml) water
½ lb (250 g) cream cheese

½ lb (250 g) cottage cheese
1 can (440 g) sweetened
   condensed milk
4 tablespoons lemon juice
1½ teaspoons grated lemon
   rind
5 passionfruit
1 cup (250 ml) cream

1. Mix together the crushed cookies, desiccated coconut and melted butter. Firmly press on the bottom of 7 × 10-inch (18 × 25-cm) tin. Chill until ready to use.
2. Mix the gelatin with the water and allow to soak for five minutes. Place over hot water and stir until dissolved.
3. Press the cream cheese and cottage cheese through a strainer. Mix the cheese together until smooth.
4. Mix in the gelatin, condensed milk, lemon juice, lemon rind and the pulp from three of the passionfruit.
5. Whip the cream and gently fold into the cheese mixture.
6. Pour over the prepared crust and spread the pulp from the remaining two passionfruit on top. Refrigerate until firm, then cut into slices.

Fruit Loaf

1 lb (500 g) cream cheese
1 cup sugar
½ cup (55 g) ground almonds
½ teaspoon almond essence
⅔ cup (80 g) chopped walnuts
1½ tablespoons rum
1 cup sliced strawberries

3 peaches, peeled and sliced
¼ cup desiccated coconut
1 cup fresh bread crumbs
2 teaspoons grated lemon rind
½ cup shredded coconut

1. Soften the cream cheese and beat in the sugar, ground almonds, almond essence, walnuts and rum.
2. Combine the strawberries and peach slices.
3. Mix together the desiccated coconut, bread crumbs and lemon rind.
4. Line a loaf tin with aluminum foil and butter lightly.
5. Sprinkle the shredded coconut on the bottom.
6. Make layers of the cream cheese mixture, fruit and bread crumb mixture. Press down slightly to make the loaf firm.
7. Cover with aluminum foil and refrigerate overnight or for several hours. Unmould and slice.

Serves 8-10.

Choc-Cheese Delights

½ lb (250 g) cooking
  chocolate
½ lb (250 g) cream cheese
⅓ cup sugar
2 egg yolks

1. Melt most of chocolate in a small bowl over hot water.
2. Spoon about a teaspoon of the melted chocolate into a paper cupcake case and tip to coat the sides. Repeat until all the chocolate is used. Chill in the refrigerator until firm.
3. Soften the cream cheese then beat in the sugar and egg yolks.
4. Spoon the cream cheese mixture into the chocolate cups.
5. Grate the remaining chocolate and sprinkle on top.

Pineapple Squares

Crust:
1½ cups crushed coconut
  cookies
½ cup (125 ml) melted butter

Filling:
½ lb (250 g) cream cheese
1 can (440 g) sweetened
  condensed milk

1 can (470 g) crushed
  pineapple
1¼ tablespoons gelatin
½ cup (125 ml) lemon juice
2 teaspoons grated lemon
  rind

1. Mix together the crushed cookies and melted butter. Press firmly on the bottom of a 7 × 10-inch (18 × 25-cm) tin. Chill until ready to use.
2. Beat together the cream cheese and condensed milk until smooth.
3. Drain the pineapple and reserve the syrup.
4. Blend the gelatin with the pineapple syrup in a saucepan and allow to soak for five minutes. Put over a low heat and stir until the gelatin is dissolved. Cool.
5. Add the gelatin mixture, lemon juice and lemon rind to the cream cheese mixture. Blend thoroughly.
6. Pour onto the prepared crust and chill until firm. Cut into squares and serve.

Sour Cream Currant Bars

Pastry:
2 cups plain flour
¾ cup (185 g) butter
4 tablespoons sugar
1 egg
1½ tablespoons sour cream

Filling:
3 eggs, separated
⅓ cup (85 g) butter
1 teaspoon vanilla essence

4 tablespoons sugar
1 tablespoon grated lemon
   rind
¾ lb (375 g) cream cheese
½ cup (125 g) sour cream
½ cup currants

1 egg yolk to glaze

1. Rub the butter into the flour until the mixture resembles fine bread crumbs. Add the sugar, egg and sour cream and mix well. If the dough is too dry, add a little cold water. Divide in half and spread one half on the bottom of a buttered 7 × 10-inch (18 × 25-cm) tin. Bake in a 350°F (180°C) oven for ten minutes. Cool.
2. Beat the egg yolks with the butter, vanilla essence, sugar, lemon rind, cream cheese and sour cream until smooth.
3. Stir in the currants.
4. Beat the egg whites until soft peaks form. Fold into the cream cheese mixture.
5. Roll out the other half of the pastry and place on top of the filling. Trim the edges and brush with the slightly beaten egg yolk.
6. Bake in a 350°F (180°C) oven for about 40 minutes. Cool and cut into bars.

Golden Yogurt Fingers

Crust:
1½ cups crushed plain
  vanilla cookies
¼ cup desiccated coconut
1¼ tablespoons honey
½ cup (125 ml) melted butter

Filling:
1 cup (250 g) yogurt

½ lb (250 g) cream cheese
4 tablespoons honey
1 teaspoon vanilla essence
1½ teaspoons grated lemon
  rind
½ cup raisins
2 teaspoons gelatin
2½ tablespoons water

1. Mix together the crushed cookies, coconut and honey mixed with the melted butter. Press firmly on the bottom of a buttered 7 × 10-inch (18 × 25-cm) tin. Chill until ready to use.
2. Beat together the yogurt, cream cheese, honey, vanilla essence and lemon rind until smooth.
3. Add the raisins and blend thoroughly.
4. Mix the gelatin with the water. Place over hot water and stir until dissolved. Stir into the yogurt mixture.
5. Pour over the prepared crust and chill until firm. Cut into fingers and serve.

Tangerine Squares

Crust:
1½ cups crushed graham
  crackers
4 tablespoons sugar
1 teaspoon cinnamon
½ cup (125 ml) melted butter

Filling:
½ lb (250 g) cream cheese

1 teaspoon grated tangerine
  rind
1 teaspoon grated lemon rind
1 can (440 g) sweetened
  condensed milk
4 tablespoons lemon juice
1½ cups chopped tangerine
  segments

1. Mix together the crushed graham crackers, sugar, cinnamon and melted butter. Press firmly on the bottom of a 7 × 10-inch (18 × 25-cm) tin. Chill until ready to use.
2. Soften the cream cheese, then mix in the tangerine and lemon rinds.
3. Beat in the condensed milk and lemon juice until smooth.
4. Fold in the chopped tangerine segments and pour onto the prepared crust.
5. Chill until firm and cut into squares.

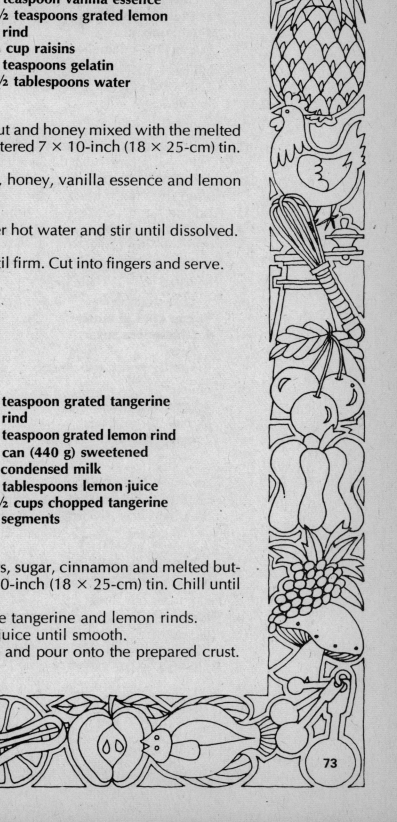

Cream Cheese Slice

Crust:
1½ cups crushed graham
   crackers
1½ teaspoons cinnamon
1 tablespoon sugar
½ cup (125 ml) melted butter

Filling:
1 lb (500 g) cream cheese
⅔ cup sugar

2½ tablespoons plain flour
4 tablespoons sour cream
1 teaspoon vanilla
⅛ teaspoon salt
1¼ tablespoons grated lemon
   rind
1¼ tablespoons lemon juice
2 eggs

1. Mix together the crushed graham crackers, cinnamon, sugar and melted butter. Press half the mixture firmly on the bottom of a 8-inch (20-cm) square tin lined with buttered wax paper.
2. Soften the cream cheese, then beat in the sugar until smooth.
3. Add the flour, sour cream, vanilla, salt, lemon rind and lemon juice.
4. Lightly beat the eggs and stir into the cream cheese mixture.
5. Pour onto the crust.
6. Sprinkle on the remaining crust mixture and press down slightly.
7. Bake in a 350°F (180°C) oven for about one hour. Cool, then chill. Cut into squares.

Tiny Cheesecake

Pastry:
1 cup (250 g) butter
½ lb (250 g) cream cheese
2 cups plain flour
¼ teaspoon salt

Filling:
6 oz (185 g) cream cheese
2½ tablespoons sugar
1 teaspoon vanilla essence
1 egg

1. Cream together the butter and cream cheese.
2. Add the flour and salt and mix well.
3. Shape into 24 small balls.
4. Press against sides and bottom of cupcake tins.
5. Mix together cream cheese, sugar, vanilla essence and egg. Spoon into pastry cups.
6. Bake in a 350°F (180°C) oven for about 20 minutes. Cool. (If desired, spread the top of each with sour cream and dot with a little jam.)

Makes 24.

Currant-Cheese Fingers

Pastry:
1½ cups plain flour
¼ lb (125 g) cream cheese
¼ lb (125 g) butter

3 tablespoons (45 g) butter
2 tablespoons sugar
1½ teaspoons cinnamon
½ teaspoon nutmeg

Filling:
1 cup (150 g) currants
2 tablespoons citron

Glaze:
1 egg white, slightly beaten
caster sugar

1. Mix together the flour, cream cheese and butter until just blended. Chill for about one hour, then roll out to a 14-inch (35-cm) square. Cut in half.
2. Combine the currants, citron, butter, sugar, cinnamon and nutmeg.
3. Spread onto one half of the pastry. Cover with the other half. Press down slightly and trim the edges. Cut into fingers.
4. Put on a buttered baking tray and glaze with the slightly beaten egg white and sprinkle with sugar.
5. Bake in a 400°F (200°C) oven for about 20 minutes.

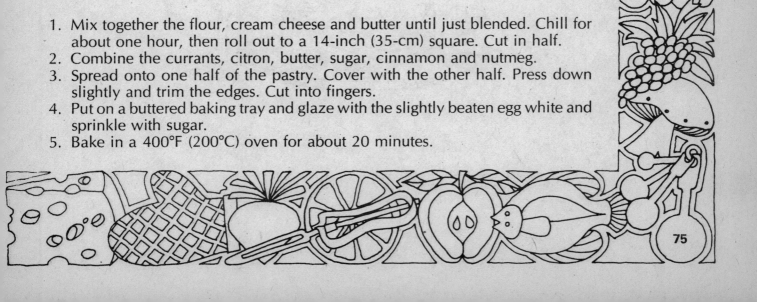

Apple Slice

Pastry:
1½ cups plain flour
½ teaspoon baking powder
½ teaspoon cinnamon
½ teaspoon nutmeg
½ teaspoon salt
4 tablespoons brown sugar
½ cup (125 g) butter
milk

Filling:
3 cooking apples
½ lb (250 g) cream cheese

½ cup sugar
3 eggs
1 can (440 g) sweetened condensed milk
½ teaspoon salt
½ cup (125 ml) lemon juice
1¼ tablespoons grated lemon rind
1 teaspoon vanilla essence
½ cup desiccated coconut
½ cup currants
1¼ tablespoons plain flour

1. Sift all the dry ingredients together into a bowl. Rub in the butter until the mixture resembles fine bread crumbs. Add just enough milk to form a firm dough. Roll out and line a 7 ×10-inch (18 × 25-cm) tin. Chill until ready to use.
2. Peel and core the apples. Cut into thin slices and arrange on the pastry.
3. Soften the cream cheese, then beat in the sugar until smooth.
4. Add the eggs one at a time, beating well after each addition.
5. Mix in the condensed milk, salt, lemon juice, lemon rind, vanilla essence, coconut, currants and flour.
6. Pour over the apples and bake in a 350°F (180°C) oven for 20 minutes. Reduce heat to 300°F (150°C) and cook for another 45 minutes. Cool, then chill. Cut into slices and serve.

Mocha Ripple Bars

Crust:
1½ cups chocolate cookie
   crumbs
1½ teaspoons instant coffee
½ cup (125 ml) melted butter

Filling:
1¼ tablespoons gelatin

½ cup (125 ml) water
1 cup sugar
1½ cups (375 ml) cream
½ lb (250 g) cream cheese
1½ teaspoons vanilla
4 tablespoons cocoa
3 teaspoons instant coffee

1. Mix together the cookie crumbs and the instant coffee. Add the melted butter and blend thoroughly. Press firmly on the bottom of a 7 × 10-inch (18 × 25-cm) tin. Chill until ready to use.
2. Soak the gelatin in the water for five minutes. Place over hot water and stir until dissolved.
3. Mix together the gelatin mixture with ½ cup sugar and ½ cup cream.
4. Soften the cream cheese and beat in the remaining sugar and the vanilla essence.
5. Add the gelatin mixture and mix well.
6. Whip the remaining cream and fold into the cheese mixture.
7. Place one third of the mixture in a small bowl and blend in the cocoa and instant coffee.
8. Alternately spoon plain and mocha mixture onto the prepared crust. Run a knife through the mixture to create a marble effect. Smooth the top. Chill overnight or for eight hours. Cut into bars.

Cottage Cheesecake Slice

Crust:
1 cup plain flour
1 cup cake flour
½ cup cornstarch
4 tablespoons custard powder
4 tablespoons confectioner's sugar
¾ cup (185 g) butter
½ cup (125 ml) water
1½ teaspoons lemon juice
1 teaspoon grated lemon rind

½ cup marmalade
egg yolk for glazing

Filling:
½ cup (125 g) butter
2 eggs, separated
4 tablespoons sugar
½ cup chopped raisins
1 teaspoon grated lemon rind
¾ lb (375 g) cottage cheese
¼ cup (65 g) sour cream
confectioner's sugar

1. Sift together the dry ingredients and rub in the butter until the mixture resembles fine bread crumbs. Add the water, lemon juice and lemon rind and mix to a firm dough.
2. Divide the dough in half and roll out one half to fit the bottom of a 7 × 10-inch (18 × 25-cm) shallow tin.
3. Spread the marmalade over the pastry.
4. Mix together the butter and egg yolks.
5. Add the sugar, raisins, lemon rind, cottage cheese and sour cream. Blend thoroughly.
6. Spread the cheese mixture over the marmalade.
7. Roll out the other half of the pastry and place on top of filling. Trim the edges and brush with the egg yolk.
8. Bake in a 350°F (180°C) oven for about 40 minutes. Cool and cut into squares. Serve sprinkled with confectioner's sugar.

Banana Cheese Slice

Pastry:
1½ cups plain flour
⅛ teaspoon salt
3 tablespoons sugar
⅓ cup (85 g) butter
1 egg

Filling:
4 tablespoons (60 g) butter
4 tablespoons sugar

2 eggs, separated
½ lb (250 g) cream cheese
4 bananas, mashed
1¼ tablespoons grated lemon rind
4 tablespoons lemon juice
½ cup raisins
milk to glaze

1. Sift together the flour, salt and sugar into a bowl. Rub in the butter until the mixture resembles fine bread crumbs. Add the egg and mix to a firm dough. Roll out ⅔ of the dough and line a buttered 7 × 10-inch (18 × 25-cm) tin. Bake the base in a 350°F (180°C) oven for ten minutes. Cool.
2. Beat together the butter and sugar until light and fluffy.
3. Add the egg yolks and beat well.
4. Soften the cream cheese and add to the mixture with the bananas, lemon rind, lemon juice and raisins. Mix thoroughly and spread over the cooled pastry.
5. Roll out the remaining pastry and cut into strips. Place in a lattice design on top of the filling.
6. Glaze with milk and bake in a 350°F (180°C) oven for 25 minutes. Cool and cut into slices.

Honey Slice

Pastry:
2 cups cake flour
⅛ teaspoon salt
2 teaspoons grated lemon
   rind
½ cup (125 ml) melted butter
1 egg
½ cup sugar
1 cup (250 ml) milk

Filling:
2 eggs, separated
½ cup sugar
¾ cup raisins
¾ lb (375 g) cottage cheese
2 teaspoons grated lemon
   rind
2½ tablespoons honey
½ cup chopped nuts

1. Sift together the flour and salt and add the grated lemon rind. Mix together the melted butter, egg, sugar and milk. Add to the flour and mix well. Spread on the bottom of a 7 × 10-inch (18 × 25-cm) tin.
2. Beat the egg yolks with the sugar until thick and creamy.
3. Stir in the raisins.
4. Press the cottage cheese through a strainer and add to the egg yolk mixture with the grated lemon rind.
5. Beat egg whites until stiff and fold into the cheese mixture.
6. Spread on top of the pastry and drip the honey over the filling. Sprinkle with chopped nuts.
7. Bake in a 350°F (180°C) oven for ½ hour. Reduce the heat to 325°F (160°C) and cook for another 15 minutes. Cool and cut into squares.

Raisin Cream Cheese Bars

Pastry:
1½ cups plain flour
½ cup custard powder
3 tablespoons confectioner's sugar
½ teaspoon baking powder
1 teaspoon cinnamon
½ cup (125 g) butter
milk

Filling:
¾ lb (375 g) cream cheese

¼ cup (65 g) butter
3 eggs
⅓ cup sugar
½ cup chopped raisins
1¼ tablespoons grated lemon rind
2 tablespoons lemon juice

1. Sift together the dry ingredients. Rub in the butter until the mixture is the consistency of fine bread crumbs. Add enough milk to form a firm dough.
2. Roll out half the dough and line the bottom of a 7×10-inch (18×25-cm) tin. Prick the pastry and bake in a 350°F (180°C) for ten minutes. Cool.
3. Soften the cream cheese and beat in the butter.
4. Beat together the eggs and sugar until thick and add to the cream cheese mixture. Mix well.
5. Add the raisins, lemon rind and lemon juice. Blend thoroughly.
6. Spread over the cooled pastry.
7. Roll out the remaining dough and place over the filling. Trim the edges and prick in several places to allow the steam to escape.
8. Bake in a 350°F (180°C) oven for about 40 minutes. Cut into bars while still warm but leave in tin to cool.

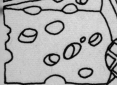

Puddings

Cherry Delight

½ lb (250 g) cream cheese
⅓ cup sugar
⅓ cup (85 ml) milk
1 can (425 g) cherries

1. Soften the cream cheese and slowly add the sugar. Beat well.
2. Add the milk and mix thoroughly.
3. Drain the cherries and remove the stones if necessary.
4. Layer the cream cheese mixture and the cherries in parfait glasses.

Serves 6.

Mocha-Cheese Souffle

4 eggs, separated	¾ cup (185 ml) water
⅔ cup sugar	3 oz (90 g) cooking chocolate
3 teaspoons instant coffee	½ teaspoon vanilla essence
½ lb (250 g) cream cheese	2 cups (500 ml) cream
2 tablespoons gelatin	ground coffee

1. Beat together the egg yolks and half the sugar until thick.
2. Add the instant coffee and mix well.
3. Soften the cream cheese and combine with the egg yolk mixture.
4. Mix the gelatin with the water and soak for five minutes.
5. Melt the chocolate and add with the vanilla essence to cream cheese mixture.
6. Put the gelatin over hot water and stir until dissolved. Stir into the cream cheese mixture.
7. Whip the cream and fold into the mixture.
8. Beat the egg whites until stiff. Slowly add the remaining sugar and continue to beat until the egg whites form stiff peaks and the sugar is dissolved. Gently fold into the cream cheese mixture.
9. Pour into a souffle dish or dessert dishes and chill until firm. Serve sprinkled with finely ground coffee.

Serves 8-10.

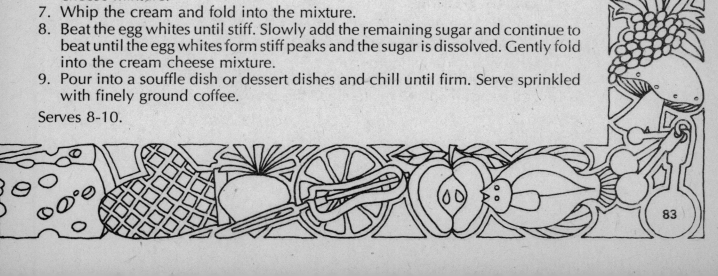

Lemon Cheese Dessert

½ lb (250 g) cream cheese
3 eggs, separated
grated rind of two lemons
½ cup (125 ml) lemon juice

1 cup (250 ml) condensed milk
4 tablespoons desiccated coconut

1. Soften cream cheese and mix in the egg yolks one at a time, beating well after each addition.
2. Thoroughly mix in lemon rind, lemon juice and condensed milk. Beat well until smooth.
3. Beat the egg whites until stiff then fold into the cream cheese mixture until thoroughly blended. Pour into a 10 × 8 inch (25 × 20 cm) dish.
4. Sprinkle on the desiccated coconut and bake in a 325°F (160°C) oven for about 45 minutes. Serve immediately.

Serves 6.

Chocolate-Cheese Roll

Cake:
1¼ cups cake flour
3 tablespoons cocoa
3 eggs, separated
½ cup sugar
3 tablespoons hot water

Filling:
½ lb (250 g) cream cheese

⅓ cup (85 ml) cream, whipped
½ cup confectioner's sugar
1 teaspoon vanila essence
confectioner's sugar

1. Sift together the flour and cocoa.
2. Beat the egg whites until stiff. Gradually add the sugar and continue beating until mixture has thickened.
3. Beat the egg yolks and add to the egg whites with the hot water and flour mixture.
4. Butter a Swiss roll tin and line with buttered wax paper. Pour in the cake mixture and bake in a 350°F (180°C) oven for about 15 minutes.
5. Turn the cake out onto a tea towel sprinkled with sugar. Peel off the wax paper and trim the crisp edges. Roll up and wrap in the tea towel. Cool.
6. Soften the cream cheese until smooth.
7. Add the whipped cream, confectioner's sugar and vanilla essence.
8. Unroll the cake and spread on the cream cheese mixture.
9. Roll up again and dust with confecioner's sugar.

Serves 6-8.

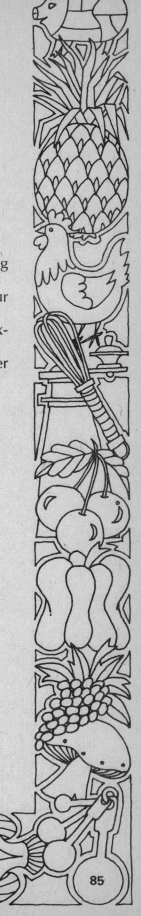

Orange-Cheese Jelly

1 pack orange jello
1 cup (250 ml) boiling water
1 cup (250 ml) orange juice
½ lb (250 g) cream cheese
1½ cups chopped orange
   segments

1 teaspoon gelatin
2½ tablespoons hot water
whipped cream

1. Mix the orange jello with the boiling water. Stir until dissolved.
2. Add the orange juice and mix well.
3. Soften the cream cheese until smooth.
4. Mix the orange pieces with the cream cheese.
5. Dissolve the gelatin in the hot water and add to the cream cheese-orange mixture.
6. Pour half the orange jello mixture into a one-quart mold. Put into the freezer until set.
7. Pour half the cream cheese-orange mixture on top and put into the freezer until set.
8. Pour on the remaining orange jello mixture and freeze until set, then pour the remaining cream cheese-orange mixture on top and set well in the refrigerator (not the freezer this time).
9. Unmold and serve with whipped cream.

Serves 4-6.

Banana Cheese Fluff

1 cup chopped
   marshmallows
⅓ cup (85 ml) milk
¼ lb (125 g) cream cheese
2 teaspoons lemon juice
2 bananas, sliced

1. Mix the marshmallows with the milk and allow to stand for ½ hour.
2. Soften the cream cheese and mix with the lemon juice.
3. Stir the sliced bananas into the cheese mixture.
4. Fold in the marshmallow mixture and spoon into dessert dishes.

Serves 4.

Blackberry Cheese Dessert

½ lb (250 g) cream cheese
2 tablespoons sugar
2 eggs, separated
1 can (425 g) blackberries,
   drained

2 cups (500 ml) cream,
   whipped
1 cup (125 g) chopped
   walnuts

1. Beat together the cream cheese and sugar until smooth.
2. Add the egg yolks one at a time, beating well after each addition.
3. Mix in the blackberries, 1½ cups of whipped cream and the walnuts.
4. Beat the egg whites until stiff and gently fold into the blackberry mixture.
5. Spoon the mixture into dessert dishes and top with the remaining whipped cream.

Serves 4-6.

Gooseberry Dessert

1 lb (500 g) gooseberries,
 peeled and sliced
¼ lb (125 g) cream cheese
½ teaspoon vanilla essence
⅓ cup sugar
¾ cup (185 ml) cream
½ cup brown sugar

1. Place the gooseberry slices in six ovenproof dishes.
2. Soften the cream cheese, then beat in the vanilla essence, sugar and ¼ cup of cream.
3. Beat the remaining ½ cup of cream and fold into the cream cheese mixture.
4. Spoon the mixture on top of the fruit.
5. Sprinkle with the brown sugar and place under a hot broiler until the sugar caramelizes. Serve warm or chilled.

Serves 6.

Banana-Cheese Dessert

1¼ tablespoons gelatin
¼ cup (65 ml) water
½ lb (250 g) cream cheese
4 bananas, mashed
1¼ tablespoons lemon juice
2½ tablespoons milk
½ cup sugar
chopped nuts

1. Mix the gelatin with the water and allow to soak for five minutes. Place over hot water and stir until dissolved.
2. Soften the cream cheese and add the dissolved gelatin, mashed bananas, lemon juice, milk and sugar. Beat well.
3. Spoon into dessert dishes and serve sprinkled with chopped nuts.

Serves 8.

Rice-Cheese Pudding

3 cups (750 ml) milk	½ cup sugar
½ cup uncooked rice	1 egg
½ cup raisins	1 teaspoon vanilla essence
¼ lb (125 g) cream cheese	½ teaspoon nutmeg

1. Heat the milk to the boiling point. Stir in the rice, cover and simmer for about 20 minutes or until the rice is tender and the milk is absorbed.
2. Soften the cream cheese and beat in the sugar, egg and vanilla essence.
3. Stir the cream cheese mixture into the rice and cook for another five minutes.
4. Serve warm or cold sprinkled with nutmeg.

Serves 4-6.

Easy Banana-Cheese Dessert

¼ lb (125 g) cream cheese
1 cup (250 ml) milk
¾ cup (185 ml) cream
4 bananas, mashed

1½ tablespoons lemon juice
½ cup sugar
1 pack instant vanilla
pudding

1. Soften the cream cheese and gradually beat in the milk and cream. Beat until smooth.
2. Stir in the bananas, lemon juice, sugar and instant pudding.
3. Spoon into dessert dishes and chill.

Serves 6-8.

Peach-Cheese Mousse

2 eggs, separated
2½ tablespoons sugar
1 can (425 g) peaches
cold milk

1¼ tablespoons cornstarch
½ lb (250 g) cream cheese
1½ tablespoons sugar
1 teaspoon cinnamon

1. Beat together the egg yolks and sugar in a saucepan.
2. Drain the peaches and measure the syrup.
3. Add enough milk to the syrup to make up to 1¼ cups (300 ml).
4. Mix the cornstarch with a little of the liquid and add to the egg yolk mixture.
5. Add the rest of the milk-syrup liquid and mix well. Stirring constantly, bring to a boil and cook for one minute.
6. Cut the peaches into small pieces and add to the mixture in the saucepan. Cool.
7. Cream the cream cheese until smooth and soft. Add the peach mixture and beat well.
8. Beat the egg whites until stiff and fold into the peach-cheese mixture.
9. Pour into dessert dishes and chill. Serve sprinkled with the sugar mixed with cinnamon.

Serves 4-6.

Cottage Cheese Pudding

½ cup dry bread crumbs
½ cup brown sugar
¼ cup (65 ml) melted butter
1 lb (500 g) cottage cheese
4 tablespoons plain flour
2 eggs, separated

½ cup sugar
1 teaspoon grated lemon rind
1¼ tablespoons lemon juice
¼ teaspoon salt
½ cup (125 ml) cream
½ cup (60 g) slivered almonds

1. Mix together the bread crumbs, brown sugar and butter. Butter a 10 × 6 × 2 inch (25 × 15 × 5 cm) baking dish and press the mixture on the bottom and half-way up the sides. Set aside.
2. Whirl the cottage cheese in an electric blender or sieve through a fine strainer. Pour into a mixing bowl.
3. Add the flour to the cottage cheese.
4. Beat the egg yolks until light yellow colored. Beat in the sugar, lemon rind, lemon juice and salt. Add to cheese mixture.
5. Beat the egg whites until stiff. Fold into the cheese mixture with the cream. Pour into baking dish.
6. Sprinkle almonds on top.
7. Bake in a 350°F (180°C) oven for 50-60 minutes. Serve warm or cold.

Serves 8.

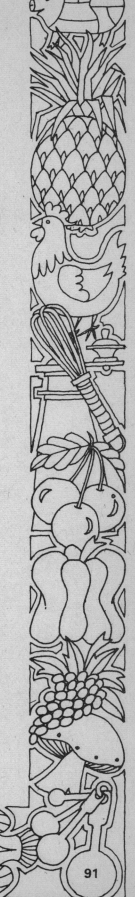

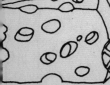

Italian Cheese Pudding

1 lb (500 g) ricotta cheese
½ cup sugar
1 cup ground almonds
6 egg whites
grated rind of one lemon
bread crumbs

1. Sieve the ricotta cheese through a fine strainer.
2. Mix together the cheese, sugar and almonds.
3. Beat the egg whites until stiff and gently fold into the cheese mixture with the grated lemon rind.
4. Pour into a buttered 1½-quart shallow cake tin. Sprinkle with bread crumbs and bake in a 350°F (180°C) oven for about ½ hour.

Serves 6.

Strawberry Ice

250 g (½ lb) cream cheese
250 g (½ lb) marshmallows
½ cup (125 ml) milk
1 cup (250 ml) cream
4 tablespoons strawberry jam

1. Beat the cream cheese until soft and smooth.
2. Mix the marshmallows with the milk in a saucepan and gently heat until the marshmallows melt. Remove from heat and cool.
3. Mix the cream with the cream cheese and pour into an ice cream tray.
4. Mix the strawberry jam with the marshmallow mixture and pour over the cream cheese mixture. Mix just a little to create a marble pattern. Put into the freezer and freeze until firm.

Serves 4-6.

Lemon Whip

2 tablespoons gelatin
¾ cup (185 ml) cold water
¾ lb (375 g) cream cheese
¾ cup sugar
⅓ cup (85 ml) milk

⅓ cup (85 ml) lemon juice
1½ cups (375 ml) cream,
  whipped
4 egg whites
grated lemon rind

1. Mix the gelatin with the cold water and allow to soak for five minutes. Place over hot water and stir until dissolved.
2. Mix the cream cheese with the sugar until soft and smooth.
3. Add the milk, lemon juice and gelatin and mix thoroughly.
4. Chill the mixture until it thickens slightly, then whip until light and fluffy.
5. Fold in the whipped cream.
6. Beat the egg whites until stiff and gently fold into the lemon mixture.
7. Spoon into dessert dishes and chill until firm.
8. Serve garnished with grated lemon rind.

Serves 6-8.

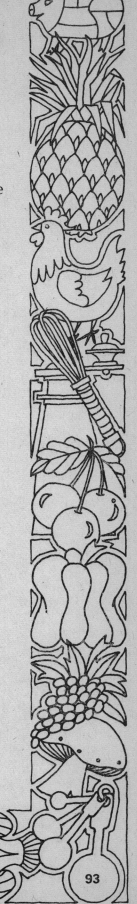

Cream Cheese Mousse

1¼ tablespoons gelatin
2½ tablespoons water
1 cup (250 ml) pineapple juice
1½ cups sugar
1 cup (250 ml) orange juice
4 tablespoons lemon juice

¾ lb (375 g) cream cheese
½ teaspoon almond extract
¼ teaspoon salt
½ cup (60 g) slivered almonds
1 cup (250 ml) cream, whipped

1. Mix the gelatin with the water and soak for five minutes.
2. Mix the pineapple juice with the sugar in a saucepan and heat.
3. Stir in the gelatin and mix until the sugar and gelatin are dissolved. Cool.
4. Add the orange and lemon juice.
5. Mix the cheese with the almond extract, salt and almonds. Stir into the gelatin mixture.
6. Fold in the whipped cream.
7. Pour into a freezing tray and freeze until firm.

Serves 8.

Index